A PRACTICAL GUIDE FOR PARENTS AND EDUCATORS

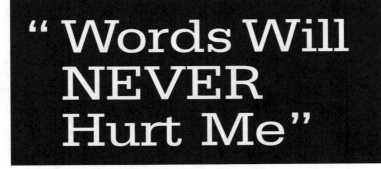

" Words Will NEVER Hurt Me "

Helping Kids Handle Teasing, Bullying and Putdowns

Written and Illustrated by
Sally Northway Ogden
www.FearFreeEd.com

A PRACTICAL GUIDE FOR PARENTS AND EDUCATORS

"Words Will NEVER Hurt Me"

Helping Kids Handle Teasing, Bullying and Putdowns

Cover and text design by Paulette Eickman

Sea Script Company

Seattle, Washington

ISBN: 978-0-9785436-6-1

Library of Congress Card Catalogue No.: 2001-090392

First Printing April 2001

Second Printing April 2004

Third Printing October 2006

Fourth Printing February 2008

Fifth Printing March 2010

Sixth Printing January 2014

Printed in Canada

Hignell Printing

Sea Script

S E A   S C R I P T   C O M P A N Y

www.seascriptcompany.com

info@seascriptcompany.com

206.748.0345

THIS BOOK IS DEDICATED TO

- *All my students of the past thirty-two years who have taught me immeasurably and given incalculable quantities of joy to my life,*

- *future students, and*

- *all those who have suffered at the hands of putdown artists, taunters, button-pushers and masters of the power of struggle.*

ACKNOWLEDGMENTS

I'd like to express my immense gratitude to *Jim Fay*, who has served as a fabulous mentor and sponsor throughout my career. You will read countless references to his wisdom and teachings throughout this book.

In addition, I am grateful to many other people who have contributed to my understanding and thus the information that is offered in this book:

Gladys Moore, deceased, transformed so many lives and will dwell forever in the hearts of those who knew her.

Carol Messmer, my loyal and compassionate friend and teacher, who shares her wisdom willingly.

Judy McLaren, my personal editor, who gives so unselfishly of her time, balancing my right-brained thoughts with skill, logic, and a wonderful sense of organization. I love to share and work with her!

Wayne Dyer, Deepak Chopra and *Shakti Gawain* contributed their fabulous quotes and spiritual Inspiration.

Foster Cline has enlightened so many and engendered so much positive change in the educational community.

Stan and *Martha Kuchel* keep me and my computer working. They are truly gifts from God!

Don Shaw, the person from whom I first heard the idea of leveling.

And, the wonderful role models of honesty and integrity who have given me a lifetime of support, direction and love; and have taught me about the nobility of diligent labor: my parents, *Ed and Florence Northway*.

Table of Contents

Preface

In 1972, I enthusiastically started my teaching career at Dunstan Junior High School. I was three months out of college and eager to teach my junior high students the intricacies and varied glories of the French language. I quickly discovered what Abraham Maslow's teachings were all about: He believed that it was next to impossible to teach children if their basic needs of feeling loved and valued weren't being met.

It was so difficult to get these adolescents to absorb the delicacies of irregular French verbs when their hearts were breaking because of something mean said to them by their peers. Most often, they had experienced a putdown. Someone had called them "dorky" or "stupid," "ugly," a "loser," a "slut," "wimpy," "weak," a "nerd," or a "geek." Often, so-called best friends reported to them that they no longer wanted to be their friends, or

bullies told them that they were going to be beaten up after school. As I drilled dialogue lines or verb conjugations, I often noticed their sullen or glazed looks. Many times tears streamed down their faces, or they just put their heads down on their desks.

That's where my problem started. I didn't know what to tell them to do! I had heard many dads tell their sons, "Go ahead and hit the guy! You don't have to take that." That violent approach seemed wrong to me, and this was certainly not a philosophy that a classroom teacher could support. (By the way, I still hear professional counselors suggest that kids who are being bullied take classes in self-defense. While I believe that self-defense can be a very valuable and noble skill to acquire, I don't think it's practical or even appropriate to use it in these types of situations. Why not learn to use our minds instead of our brawn?)

I remembered from my experience in school that we were told to ignore this type of behavior ... but I didn't recall that ignoring behaviors was particularly successful, either. It only worked occasionally, and many times it failed miserably. "Retaliate!" "Don't get mad; get even!" Now, *there* was an option, and a good solid American doctrine. However, I had been taught not to "sink to the level of the other person." Also, I subscribed to Gandhi's statement:

"An eye for an eye leaves everyone blind."

I couldn't find any books specifically on the subject of how to handle putdowns and criticism, and the topic was not covered in my college psychology classes, even though I've heard it estimated that the average student will hear 150,000 putdowns before his graduation from high school (though not all of them are directed at him). The National Association of School Psychologists reports that currently one in seven students in America is either a bully or the victim of one! In February 2001, Attorney General Ken Salazar was quoted in Colorado's *Rocky Mountain News* as saying that bullying was a significant problem for schools. After hearing results from statewide school meetings scheduled in response to the Columbine tragedy, he estimated that 10,000 youngsters in Colorado miss at least one day of school each month because they're afraid to go to school due to bullying.

Several years ago I met a principal at Jim Fay's conference in

Copper Mountain, Colorado, who polled his elementary school students every year. He asked them to list the five toughest things about going to elementary school. Every year they consistently listed the following five things as the most difficult aspects of being an elementary student:

1. being called names
2. getting along with people you don't like
3. handling rumors
4. wearing the right clothes
5. feeling accepted by the group

It's obvious that kids need help handling these issues and learning to feel good about themselves, even in elementary school. Isn't it interesting that none of these stressors has anything to do with academic accomplishments?

I began a quest to understand why putdown situations occurred, and how the "putdown-ees" could respond and react differently without becoming so wounded. Because regardless of the old adage, "Sticks and stones may break my bones, but words will never hurt me," my observation was that *words in fact did hurt!* The students needed some new solutions. And for many of them, it was important that they break the cycle of being perpetually abused. I talked with my friends, students, colleagues, school counselors, professional counselors, and college professors. I got my Master of Arts degree in Curriculum and Instruction, and I looked for answers in films and books of all kinds.

This book offers a summary of the information I have gathered from these sources throughout these past twenty-nine years. I have written it using the style I use when I present this material to my students. I hope that teachers or parents will find that the concrete explanations are helpful to use with their students and children. In the first chapter, you will meet Cletis and Beatrice. They represent an oversimplified and exaggerated way to communicate an advanced concept to concrete thinkers. Most people, young or adult, can relate to this example.

I have been teaching for the last sixteen years at Chatfield Senior High School in Littleton, Colorado. On April 20, 1999, Eric Harris and Dylan Klebold willfully killed one teacher, twelve of their classmates and themselves at Columbine High School. Columbine and Chatfield are neighboring schools. Chatfield students have grown up with Columbine students, sharing the same shopping malls, church groups, recreational facilities and activities. Thus, we were profoundly affected by the tragedy and very involved in its aftermath. Many sources cited that part of Harris and Klebold's motivation for the shooting was revenge for the tauntings and putdowns that they had experienced at school. I couldn't help but wonder whether this atrocity could have been prevented if they had known and applied the information contained in this book.

As a result of the monstrous tragedy at Columbine, many schools are searching for and implementing programs to stop violence. I suggest that in every program, in order for it to be effective, there should be a component of teaching kids how to *think differently* about aggressive and insulting behavior directed toward them. Then, if we arm them with *skills*, kids will depend on adults to protect them only in the most serious of cases. I truly believe that most violent situations could be averted by teaching youngsters how to respond appropriately and in a healthy manner from the beginning.

Even though the ideas I offer are simplified and practical, the true answer to this situation is more difficult. As a society, I believe that we need to find ways of teaching children to love themselves ... so deeply and unconditionally that they are never inclined to hurt others in order to alleviate their own pain or fear. They would then grow into adults with whom it would be easy to work, live and interact. Sadly, until all of our institutions have dedicated themselves to this end, it will probably be a necessity to teach children (and adults) how to interpret and respond to mean criticism, putdowns, cruel acts, taunting, and violence.

Whereas the Columbine tragedy brought tremendous attention to this topic, I believe that the question of what to do about man's inhumanity to man is universal and timeless. If children gathered together thousands of years ago in cave schools, some of them probably threw stones and uttered mean messages to other children. Peer cruelty has been an issue throughout my thirty years in the classroom. I expect that humans' brutality to one another will continue to some degree, so the information presented in this book will be of value for many years in the future. It's time, however, to improve the understandings, skills, and attitudes of kids so that they can become empowered to handle the criticism and harrassment they receive appropriately and compassionately.

I focus primarily on true putdowns rather than on teasing, which has been misinterpreted. There is a great deal of teasing and name calling, especially in the schools, which is friendly and loving in its intent. I notice this on television sitcoms, too. However, frequently people interpret an attempt to play or tease as a putdown. This misinterpretation is commonplace among highly sensitive adolescents. I believe it just takes some experience to learn the difference between a tease and a putdown. A strong self-concept will help a person to distinguish between the two as well. One who believes in himself does not personalize or feel insulted by every comment that is directed his way. He can roll with the punches. In fact, I see students with strong self-esteem *automatically assume* that the person is kidding and respond accordingly. Even if the person was serious, this can be a great way to diffuse the putdown!

The material in this book can help to teach young people how to handle difficult situations and toxic people so that their self-concepts stay strong, and so that they avoid violence and engaging in nasty behavior. The better kids feel about themselves, the better they will feel toward their classmates and the more they can direct their attention toward learning. In addition, they can begin to feel more peace of mind and experience more joy in a variety of situations. Then teaching could return to what I had envisioned in the "teaching brochure": a classroom where kids like themselves, one another, and learning!

When I started presenting this information to teacher and parent groups, I discovered that it was very well received, because adults also have a tremendous need for these understandings. Parents are eager to know what to tell their children who face bullying and taunting in the classroom. And unfortunately, putdowns and power struggles are common throughout society.

Evidently there are difficult and critical people not only in the classroom, but also in the workplace, at social gatherings, and scattered throughout society. I wonder how many nasty comments are heard in Hollywood? Or in the Army? On the construction site? I truly believe that people of all ages and professions can benefit from the concepts introduced in this book. My hope is that they will read, digest, practice, and apply the information presented in this book so that they can truly say to themselves, ***"Words will NEVER hurt me!"***

In order not to detract from the central message of the text, the pronouns "he," "him" and "himself" are used to respectfully denote both genders.

Why Putdowns Happen

Cletis is a high school boy who has been making choices that have turned out to be problematic for him. He has neglected his chores and has saved little of his earnings from his after-school job, instead he spends his money on compact discs and his time on video games. His girlfriend is unhappy that he calls her so rarely, and his grades are slipping in school, because he hasn't been disciplined enough to do his homework consistently. One day, on his way to work, his car runs out of gas. Figures. He forgot to get gas the day before, and didn't have any money, anyway. He walks the rest of the way to work, arriving very late. His boss, furious that he is late for the third time that week, fires him on the spot. Bummer. He returns home to find his mother upset with him, too. He hasn't done his chores all week. As a consequence, his mom lowers his allowance for the next two weeks, and instructs him to make his own dinner. He grabs a hot dog and goes upstairs to do his homework and to arrange for a ride to school the next day. He gets hooked watching a sporting event on television, then falls asleep. He wakes up that night in time to write a composition for his English class, albeit hurriedly. He gets to bed late and wakes up late the next morning. His mom reminds him to take out the trash. In his tired fog, he takes out the trash and departs on his bike for school, having forgotten to call a friend for a ride. He arrives at school and meets his friends in the hall. "You're in trouble, Cletis. Seems that your girlfriend is going out with Joe Cool Saturday night. She says she's tired of you not calling her." What else could go wrong, Cletis wonders. He goes to class, only to discover that the paper he wrote for English is not in his notebook. He must have accidentally thrown it away with the trash!

Imagine what the day is like for Cletis. Does he concentrate on his work? Does he disrupt class, or is he attentive? Is he friendly and outgoing to his classmates? There is a new student in one of his classes; does he introduce himself? Is he helpful to his teachers and friends? If an underclassman steps in front of him in the lunch line, what is he likely to do?

Most people agree that under these circumstances, the behavior we would see from Cletis would be less than ideal! He is likely to disrupt or not attend class, pout, stick to himself, and be generally nasty to all. He might even get in a fight with the underclassman who stepped in front of him in the lunch line! Unfortunately, most of us can relate to Cletis, because we have experienced terrible days like this.

Sigmund Freud called this behavior "displacement," a defense mechanism used by people who are feeling anxious or inadequate. They displace the frustration from one situation to another. For example, Cletis has a bad day, so he takes it out on others. Dad has a tough time at work, so he comes home and yells at his child or kicks the dog. A teacher has a fight with her husband before school and snaps at her first period class. Battering of women increases in cities where the home football team loses! Unfortunately, this is a very common way that people respond to problems. A much more acceptable way of dealing with these situations is to identify the true feelings and to talk openly about them.

By contrast, Beatrice is having a very different experience. (By the way, a seventh grader looked at a list of French names for girls and said, "Beet-Rice, what kind of a name is Beet-Rice?" So I continue to use the name, and its correct pronunciation in this context is "Beet-Rice.") She has decided to make some personal growth. She is going to turn over a new leaf. She goes in for extra help in math class and has decided to do her chores, then her homework, immediately upon her return from school. Her parents are delighted that she has been doing her chores, so they reward her with a large increase in allowance. She has decided that she needs to be more outgoing with boys and takes the risk of talking with a boy she has had a crush on for a while. She has been really concentrating at work, too, and her boss has given her an increase in salary. She gets to school the next day and discovers that her math grade has improved from a C- to a B+. Her girlfriends have invited her to go shopping that weekend. The boy she has had a crush on asks her if she would like to go out Saturday night!

Imagine what this day will be like for Beatrice. How will she act in class? Will she be attentive and industrious? Will she be outgoing or introverted? Is she likely to introduce herself to a new student? If an underclassman steps in front of her in the lunch line, what is she likely to do? Is she helpful and friendly to teachers and peers, or does she stick to herself?

Most people will agree that Beatrice will be friendly, outgoing, and industrious on this day. She is likely to be helpful to her teachers and classmates. She might very well extend herself to a new student and is likely to allow the underclassman to butt in line and think little of it. Fortunately, most of us can relate to great days like this one, too!

These stories of Cletis and Beatrice are designed to prove the point that Dr. Wayne Dyer makes in his book *Real Magic:*

> **"How I am treating others is essentially how I am treating myself, and vice versa."**

This means that the way I see myself is translated into my behavior. If I am talking to myself as a critical parent would, I tend to speak to others in the same critical tone. If I am angry at myself, as Cletis undoubtedly is, I am likely to be angry and intolerant of others. If I am pleased with myself, as Beatrice is, I am likely to be pleasant and compassionate with others. Therefore, when I criticize others, this behavior likely stems from criticism of myself. A poor self-concept can take many forms of poor behavior. It may manifest itself as a desire to control, to gain power over, or be superior to others. People who love themselves unconditionally are not caustic, violent, or fault-finding of others. Great examples include Jesus, Buddha, Gandhi, and Mother Teresa. You just don't hear stories of these people being aggressive or nasty toward others! By contrast, the great villains of history are not noted for their blessed childhoods or deep feelings of self-love.

Abraham Lincoln summed up this concept this way:

"When I do good, I feel good.
When I do bad, I feel bad."

Howard C. Cutler, M.D., quoted His Holiness the Dalai Lama as saying virtually the same thing as Lincoln, but explained in more detail:

Survey after survey has shown that it is unhappy people who tend to be most self-focused and are often socially withdrawn, brooding, and even antagonistic. Happy people, in contrast, are generally found to be more sociable, flexible, and creative and are able to tolerate life's daily frustrations more easily than unhappy people. And most important, they are found to be more loving and forgiving than unhappy people.

Tremendous power lies in learning how to translate the cruel actions and words of people from the overt message to the covert message, or from the open and obvious statement to the hidden one beneath it. Management guru Peter Drucker said:

"The important thing in communication is to hear what isn't being said."

When we understand that a person's behavior is a direct reflection of how he sees himself at the moment of the behavior, we can interpret his message differently and more accurately. Then, we can choose from an entirely different repertoire of responses. However, sometimes it is hard to convince people that Cletis, for example, is not feeling good about himself when he criticizes others. It is often difficult for people to see that a Cletis type is not feeling good about himself for these reasons:

1. Cletis may look very good from the outside. He may be handsome, muscular and well-dressed. It is often difficult for people in this society to see beyond external appearances. Many Americans have had a difficult time understanding why so-called beautiful people like Elvis, Marilyn Monroe and Princess Diana were unhappy. However, it's impossible to determine, by looking at exteriors, how someone is feeling about himself inside. What's the best way to find out how he feels inside? By looking at his behavior.

2. One's self-concept changes, depending on the situation. Cletis may be the captain of the football team, and he may feel very confident about that position. In that situation, he may appear to be a star, and because he feels comfortable and capable, he may be very compassionate and patient with others. However, he may have had a very different set of experiences in math class and feel inadequate or threatened in that setting. He is more likely to be critical of others, especially the teacher, in math class! Americans had a difficult time understanding how O.J. Simpson could have been a wife abuser, because they perceived him to be a successful professional athlete and actor. Clearly, he felt relatively confident in those arenas. However, in the area of interpersonal relationships, his feelings of inadequacy were obviously much greater. Most people's self-concept varies greatly, depending on the situation in which they find themselves. Most feel one way at a party, another way at the top of a difficult ski slope, and still another way before giving a speech to a large group.

In the situation at Columbine, it was probably very difficult for Harris and Klebold to understand that the kids who were taunting them had problems themselves. Why? Because these taunters were reported to be the athletes, the ones perceived to be "in power" at the school. But just because a kid is a standout on the football field, that doesn't mean he feels great about himself in English class, or at home with a step-mom. But to a child who longed to be in power or to be a football star, this reality was probably very difficult to understand. What's ironic is that both Harris and Klebold were good students. They probably didn't understand that some kids who struggled with their schoolwork were likely to be jealous of them because of their ease with academics.

3. Many Americans have a misconception about stuck-up or conceited behavior. They have been taught to believe that people who act stuck-up truly think they are too good for others. Cletis is likely to appear conceited on his bad day described earlier, because he isn't outgoing or friendly to others ... and he looks good on the outside. Actually, the opposite is true. People who act conceited (or superior to others) do not really believe that they are better than others. If they felt loving toward themselves, they would act that way toward others. Why do others interpret Cletis' behavior to be conceited? Because they are not looking deeply enough at what is going on with him. They are falling for the externals. And often, people who are feeling insecure have learned to use deceit to their advantage. It's a way for them to cover up what is really going on inside of them. It is difficult for people in this culture, especially males, to tell the truth about what they are feeling. An emotionally healthy Cletis would tell his friends, "I'm not feeling too good about myself right now. I've made some bad choices and have experienced some difficult consequences as a result. My parents, boss, and girlfriend are all fed up with me. I'm feeling really inadequate." Instead, he keeps this to himself, walks by and ignores his friends, and appears stuck-up. That's not all bad for Cletis, because that way he covers perfectly for what is really going on inside!

This stuck-up behavior may be deliberate or accidental, a conscious or unconscious choice. But either way, there is often a big pay off! Many people are fooled and distracted from the real issues going on with the person, so he doesn't have to reveal his weakness or the source of his pain. Freud explained this conceited behavior as the defense mechanism "reaction formation," meaning that the individual behaves in an exaggerated way that is in direct opposition to how he really feels. For example, he feels weak, so he acts as if he is strong (perhaps by being aggressive or attempting to control others). He might hate someone, so he is overly condescending and attentive to the person. Often, people who are sexually frustrated tell dirty jokes and act "macho" or sexy. Shakespeare said, "Me thinks thou doth protest too much," meaning that the more a person protests or defends himself, the more he casts guilt upon himself. Therefore, the more conceited a person appears, the more inadequate he probably feels.

If the way we treat others is a reflection of how we treat ourselves, then it is impossible to love ourselves too much. The more we love ourselves, the more loving we will act toward others. Conceited behavior is not loving. Therefore, it is not a reflection of someone who loves himself too much, but rather too little.

4. We tend to concentrate on our own weaknesses, while overlooking the weaknesses of others. We tend to see the strong and wonderful qualities of our friends and colleagues. We see what is good about Cletis, but we don't know what issues he's struggling with. Most people, sadly, tend to focus on their own weaknesses, and not applaud themselves for their strengths. Ironically, we've been taught that if we remember our best qualities, we'll get a "big head!" This is, of course, untrue, and most growth comes from building on our strengths, not our weaknesses!

I learned this many years ago, when I was an active racquetball player. I had a friend named Laurie who was a wonderful racquetball player and a very beautiful woman, with a figure that was widely admired. I have always battled with an extra ten or twenty pounds, and have never thought of myself as being particularly athletic. Laurie was my hero! She had two qualities I strived to attain, a great figure and wonderful athletic talent. One day in the locker room, she said to me, "You know Sally, maybe you could be attractive if you lost some weight!" Whew! What a putdown! I was really hurt, and because I saw her strengths through the eyes of what I valued, I could not imagine why she would need to put me down. I reflected on it and discovered her area of weakness. She didn't have many friends and I did! She was envious of the many good friendships that I had, and wasn't reflecting at the time on two of her strengths, being a great racquetball player or having a wonderful figure. She appeared stuck-up to others, but I learned that her behavior was really coming from an area in which she did not feel loving toward herself.

A problem with teaching young people to deal with putdowns is that many of them have such a poor self-concept that they just believe the surface message. Why? Because they see so many other people as being better or more valuable than they are and believe that they are bad or unlovable. It's hard for them to see that the putdown is a reflection of the *other person's lack of belief in himself*, because they believe that the putdown is true! They concentrate on their own weaknesses and have a difficult time seeing that others may feel badly about themselves, too!

Most people base their judgment of themselves on their *weaknesses*, while valuing others for their *strengths*.

TEACHER: (In private to Susie after class) Susie, you didn't seem like yourself in class today. Is something going on with you?

SUSIE: Yeah ...

TEACHER: What's going on?

SUSIE: I don't know ...

TEACHER: Is it something with your friends, parents, grades, teachers, or ... ?

SUSIE: It's just everything.

TEACHER: Which would you say is the most troublesome? Friends, parents, grades, teachers ... ?

SUSIE: Well, it just seems like my best friend is really mean to me lately, and it's so hard because she's in all my classes. And we've been best friends forever!

TEACHER: Oh, I'm sorry to hear that. It must be tough to come to school when you aren't getting along with your best friend!

SUSIE: Yeah.

TEACHER: Is it something happening with her? What do you think has happened?

SUSIE: I don't know. I haven't done anything!

TEACHER: I bet you haven't! I was wondering if you can think of anything that's going on in her life aside from your relationship.

SUSIE: Well, her mom and dad are separating, but I've been really good at listening to her talk about it. And she says she's handling it just fine. But then she's mean to me!

TEACHER: That's really nice that you've been so helpful to her. I bet it's confusing to you that she's been mean to you in return. Would you like my guess on what's happening?

SUSIE: Sure.

TEACHER: Well, what I've learned over the years is that the way people behave has a lot more to do with what's going on in their lives than what we have done to them. Have you ever had a day when you feel really badly about life? You know, one of those days when everything goes wrong?

SUSIE: Yeah ...

TEACHER: We all have those sometimes. How did you act to other people? Were you real friendly, or did you pout and snap at people or ... ?

SUSIE: I think I pouted and snapped. I don't think I am very nice when everything goes wrong ...

TEACHER: Exactly! Well, you're like many people. It seems pretty likely to me that is what is going on with her. I bet she is really struggling with her parents' split and isn't able to leave her sadness and fear out of her reaction to others.

SUSIE: But she looks like she's doing fine!

TEACHER: That's the tricky part. People often look good on the outside to cover up what is really going on with them inside. But the real way we know is not how the other guy looks, but how he behaves!

SUSIE: But she has so much going for her, I just figured she'd handle this fine. I was thinking that I must have done something wrong.

TEACHER: Most of us tend to concentrate on what we're doing wrong and not see what's happening with the other guy. Sometimes we aren't even doing anything wrong. But the way we can always tell is by looking at the other guy's behavior. People who feel good about themselves treat other people well. People who aren't doing so great don't treat other people well. As far as I know, there just aren't any exceptions to that.

SUSIE: Yeah, but she used to be really nice to me!

TEACHER: Yep, and I bet at that time she didn't feel so scared. How we feel about ourselves can change because the situations we find ourselves in change, too. In some of them we feel really confident and happy, but in others, we feel scared and inadequate. I don't know exactly what is troubling her, but I can guarantee you that if she is being mean to you at this time, something about her isn't doing well right now ...

SUSIE: I guess I can see that ... I really don't think I have done anything wrong.

TEACHER: I bet you haven't!

SUSIE: Thanks ... this will help me be more understanding of what she is going through, and not feel so badly about myself.

TEACHER: If you'd like some ideas on what to say when she says mean things to you, feel free to stop by. I have some great things you can try.

SUSIE: Thanks! Just knowing that it isn't me has been really helpful. I feel better about the whole deal now.

Leveling

eveling is another way to describe to people why putdowns happen. Think of the "perfect" person as a 10. Then assign yourself a "score" between 1 and 10. Remember this score. Now, think of your best friend, mate, or dearly beloved. Assign him or her a score between 1 and 10. Next, think of one of your least favorite people. This is someone you really don't like to be with, or someone around whom you feel very nervous or anxious. Assign him or her a score between 1 and 10. Let's compare scores. First, subtract the score of your favorite person from your score. Next, subtract from your score that of the individual with whom you're not comfortable. What is the difference in the scores in each case? Most people report (and I have asked literally thousands of them in my conferences and presentations) that there is only a point or two of difference between their score and that of their favorite person. However, there tends to be 3 to 6 points difference between their score and that of their least favorite person.

What does this prove? Most people tend to hang around people who score very close to themselves. They like to spend time with people they see as being on about the same level as they are. This is what is easiest and most comfortable for most people. They tend to avoid people they see as "beneath" them, because they feel these people aren't challenging or exciting to be with. By contrast, they may feel inadequate in the company of people they see as too much "above" them. Since this is so difficult for most people to handle, they look for a way to make things level. There are two ways to do this. One way is to raise their own score by concentrating on and applauding themselves for their own fine qualities. Unfortunately, this seems to be a reaction that is not most commonly chosen. The other way takes less thinking, is more expedient, and is more often modeled in society. That solution to leveling the scores is to put the other person down. This way, they can lower the score of the other guy to their level, making things less stressful for themselves.

The concept of leveling is a simple way to help understand what often happens in relationships. You will sometimes hear people explain their divorces by saying, "We grew apart." I believe that often one person grows and the other does not, and the difference in the two scores causes difficulties that many times cannot be surmounted.

Suppose my husband and I are both movie stars. He makes a hit movie, while I have been without a starring role for a year. What happens? His score goes shooting up, while mine stays at the same level as it was before his hit movie. My score could even go down. The discrepancy in these scores has the potential of causing big problems for us.

Remember, there are two possibilities. We can find ways to make ourselves feel proud and adequate, thereby raising our own score, or we can put down the other person. Which is easier and more prevalent? Right! Putting the other guy down is the quicker way to level out the scores so people can feel comfortable again.

I believe it is sad that people tend to judge others so much. Very often the judgments are based on ridiculous or superficial attributes. But since judging occurs so often in our society, we should understand how it all works. Then, let's learn to get beyond this detrimental judging and criticizing of others!

An example that most of us can relate to is the selection of high school cheerleaders. Let's say that you and I both try out to be cheerleader. You make it, I don't. Immediately, because being a cheerleader is something I value, your score goes shooting up. I feel uncomfortable. I need to get the scores more level. Again, I have two choices. I can attempt to raise mine, or lower yours. I could highlight my strengths in my own mind and remember that it's okay to have weaknesses and to be rejected, both are part of the human condition. I could remind myself of my other talents, the friends I have, and the growth I have made in my life. I could choose to believe that there are many other ways that I could participate in and enjoy the high school experience. Or, I could put you down. I could say that you wear too much make-up, that you just tried out so that you could wear the short skirts (which may have appealed to me, too), and I could call you a "bitch," "slut," or worse. Which seems to occur more frequently? The self-affirmation, or the putdown? It's pretty obvious that the putdown is the more commonly chosen route to leveling our scores and getting to where I feel somewhat better about the situation.

I learned this lesson in a powerful way the year that I was selected as Colorado Teacher of the Year. I was completely thrilled and delighted, but at the same time I felt overwhelmed, baffled and amazed by the selection. I had only been teaching for five years, and I could think of countless areas of weakness in my teaching. Many people were quick to congratulate and celebrate the honor with me, but some of my other colleagues were not so kind. They went to extremes to point out my inadequacies, mentioning things that were true and other things that were untrue. Because I didn't understand the concept of leveling, it was very hurtful to me at the time. Now I understand that this discrepancy in the scores was very difficult for them to handle. The way they found to deal with their pain was to attack and criticize me. This was especially difficult for me, because I believed much of what they had to say! As most people do, I wasn't concentrating on my wonderful qualities. I was thinking about all of my weaknesses and wondering, "How could they award such an honor to a person who still has so much growing to do?"

Remember that many people are inclined to base their judgments of themselves on their inadequacies, concentrating on the areas that bother them or they need to improve. They tend to overlook their strengths and take their assets for granted. But when they look at others, they tend to see what they are good at, what is beautiful about them, their skills and talents. They don't know what the other guys worry about before they go to sleep at night! I don't know what causes them pain, what they struggle with, what they fear. I don't notice if they have gained five pounds or spent too much money last month. I don't know how they are getting along with their spouse and children. I don't know if they are trying to conquer an addiction or are frustrated about having a poor relationship with their mother-in-law. And, of course, most people are very good at covering up these things.

However, when I look at myself, I know what my own battles are. And that's what I tend to concentrate on. When I'm going through tough times, I don't find myself saying, "Yes, but remember, you're trilingual." Kids don't usually say to themselves, "My friends are saying mean things about me, but it doesn't matter much because I'm so good in math and have pretty blue eyes."

Great evidence of this can be seen in how many movie stars don't see themselves as particularly attractive or special. Kelly McGillis, the female heartthrob in the movie *Top Gun*, reportedly will not look at herself in a mirror because she believes that she is so ugly! Minnie Driver, the gorgeous love interest in the movie *Good Will Hunting*, is quoted in *Cosmopolitan* as saying, "I swear to God, I would marry the first person who asked me, just because it seems so impossible that anyone would ask."

Burt Reynolds, once a Hollywood sex idol, was asked whom he would choose to be with if he were stranded on a desert island. He said that he would pick Dinah Shore. When asked why, he answered that she made him feel like a handsome and worthwhile man. It's hard to imagine that such an acclaimed movie star needed someone else to assure him that he was attractive. He must have been overlooking his assets that the rest of the country regularly applauded him for.

Sadly, but usually true, people tend to concentrate on their own weaknesses and others' strengths. That's why it was so difficult for me to deal with the criticism I received after I was chosen to be the Colorado Teacher of the Year. It was hard for me to change my perspective and see that it was really about my colleagues' jealousy because I believed much of what they were saying.

In addition, so often we are unaware of how others see us relative to the issues that make them feel inadequate. For example, I had a roommate who was not a college graduate. Since I am a school teacher, and most of my friends are teachers, too, we are all college graduates. My roommate had a very difficult time being around us. I eventually discovered that she felt inadequate not having a college degree. She would find other things to criticize in an attempt to level the scores. It took me a while to understand that her criticisms about other issues really stemmed from the fact that she judged herself as less of a person around college graduates, and that she needed to find a way to raise her score in other arenas. Why was this so tough to figure out? Because I didn't give a second thought to having finished college. This was not a big deal to me at all. It was only a big deal to *her* because she hadn't.

I heard the story once of a beautiful, wise and well-traveled woman who lost her hair after a bout with cancer. She was invited one evening to a party at the United Nations in New York with her son. Her son was proud to be with her. Though she was in her seventies, she was an articulate, elegant and very attractive woman whom other guests at the gala found charming and interesting. She wore an expensive wig to cover her hair loss. At the end of the evening, her son said, "Mom, I was so proud to be with you! Other guests were so complimentary of your grace, beauty and wisdom. What were your thoughts on the party?" His mother responded, "Well, I had a lovely time, but did you notice how many women had gorgeous, thick, beautiful hair?"

Isn't it interesting, with all the marvelous traits this woman possessed, that she should concentrate on her one weakness: her loss of hair? And isn't it likely, as well, that the other guests didn't even notice her wig, nor understand that she might be looking at *their* hair? It is almost impossible to know through what psychological lenses others really see us, or to understand on what basis they see and judge themselves!

In addition, sadly, in our society, there seems to be an unstated belief that if you do well, I can't be doing well, too! A highly competitive individual not only needs to level the scores but also needs to get his above yours. This competition undermines and destroys many relationships. Gore Vidal stated,

"Every time a friend succeeds, I die a little."

Sad, isn't it? Just because a friend succeeds, that doesn't mean we failed! George Carlin gives this concept another slant,

"It isn't enough that I do well; others have to do poorly."

Lord Chesterfield adds,

"Most people enjoy the inferiority of their friends."

A strong, healthy person can celebrate his friends' successes as well as his own! Unfortunately, because putdowns still abound throughout society, it's apparent that many people still are not emotionally healthy enough to be capable of sharing in the joy of the success and happiness of others.

Dr. Wayne Dyer sums it up beautifully:

"When we highlight the weaknesses of others, we praise ourselves."

I have a friend who has a beautiful home in the mountains— rock fireplaces, swimming pool, greenhouse, wooden floors, and decks off the master bedroom. I live in a cozy, smallish home in the suburbs. When I saw Cindy's house, her score went shooting up. So I found myself saying, "Yes, but how do you drive these snowy roads in the winter?" "Who washes all these windows?" "Isn't heating a greenhouse expensive?" "And how about maintaining the chemical balances in the swimming pool and hot tubs?" "Isn't that a lot of work?" With each criticism, by pointing out the negative, I was "lowering" her house, bringing the score closer to the score I had given to my house. When I got home I felt great about not having to do all the work that came with her gorgeous house!

Listen to women talk about cover girls! They will say many mean things, designed to help themselves feel better about not being as beautiful as the models. Examples? "It's all silicone." "It's airbrushed." "I'd like to see her when she's forty and has had a couple of kids." "She's probably really stupid; I bet she can't put a sentence together."

Bernard Berenson, a Lithuanian-American art critic and author stated:

> **"Life has taught me that it is not for our faults that we are disliked and even hated, but for our qualities."**

I have a friend who recently lost 40 pounds. What was the response to her tremendous weight loss? "Yes, I know she's lost 40 pounds, but don't you think her face looks a little drawn?" "How will she afford all new clothes and alterations? I wouldn't want those bills!" "It isn't healthy to lose weight that quickly, is it?"

Actually, a great deal of peer pressure is related to this concept of leveling. Let's say you and I are adolescents at a party where alcohol is being served. You show self discipline and decline a beer when it's offered. I've already accepted one. Your score goes up, while mine slides (although I might not ever be honest enough to admit this). I say, "Well what a party pooper you are! What a dud! Are you going to go through all of life and be a fuddy-duddy and a geek? Gosh … what a loser!"

My dad had a beautiful Lincoln Mark III that a friend of his criticized until the day he purchased it from my dad. Then it became the best car on the road! Examples like these abound.

I had a student who was exceptionally beautiful. She was selected as ninth-grade homecoming attendant. I asked her during Homecoming Week if she was enjoying all the fun and attention. "Are you kidding?" she asked. "This week has been hell!" I asked her what had been going on. She answered that many of her friends had turned on her. They had started criticizing her boyfriend, telling her that she wore too much make-up, saying she wasn't pretty at all, one "friend" had even called her a "slut," etc., etc. It was a clear case of leveling. These girls were obviously jealous of her newfound fame and attention.

This was especially hurtful for her, because she believed many of their criticisms! She did not look in the mirror and say to herself, "Gosh, I'm pretty!" Few ninth-grade girls do! Instead, most adolescent girls (and many adults of both sexes) concentrate on a new pimple, or think their noses are too big, or think their hair is too thick, thin, curly or straight! Remember, most people concentrate on their own inadequacies, while seeing primarily the strengths of others. That's often why it's so hard for people to change their perspective and see that the putdown is really *about the other guy!*

I experienced another example of this incongruity just recently. A very handsome senior boy came to talk to me because he was frustrated that he didn't have the courage to ask cute girls on dates. I found this very surprising, because I saw him as a confident, attractive, fun boy. I even knew of several girls who had crushes on him. After I finished talking with him, a very popular girl, who had seen me talking to him, came up to me and said, "I just think he's the "hottest" guy I've ever seen! I wish someone like that would ask me out someday ... but I doubt it will happen. Well, I can dream, anyway ..." I had been trying, in vain, to convince the boy that others saw him this way!

There are many reasons why people use putdowns or opt to get into power struggles. But all of the reasons explain more about the psychological make-up of the person inciting the mean or critical behavior than about the person receiving the putdowns. Displacement, reaction formation, and leveling are probably the most common reasons why, but these take many forms. In general, the putdown fills a need for the sender ... a need to feel powerful, to protect himself, to be in control, to feel important or to garner applause.

Dr. Wayne Dyer says it well:

When we criticize others, we do not define them; we define ourselves.

Some people use putdowns in order to impress other people, or to look tough and strong ... they've discovered that the best defense is a good offense. If the putdown artist calls you a loser first, maybe you won't guess that he feels like one sometimes, too. He might be wanting to cover up a weakness in this way. He could be hurt. Or sad. He might be having a bad day, like Cletis. Maybe someone just put *him* down!

Maybe his parents have always been critical of him, and that's how he's learned to interact with his peers. Maybe he feels powerless, so he needs to get some power from you. If he can get you to look, or better yet, *act* like an idiot, what a quick power fix for him! Or maybe he thrives on attention, whether it's positive or negative. Maybe he's trying to "stir something up." Maybe he feels he can gain some level of acceptance from some group of people. Maybe he's just a very negative person, criticizing everyone. Maybe he's angry at someone else, and you just happen to be handy. Maybe he has to try to gain control of others all the time.

But whatever the specific reason, if you're being put down, remember, *it's really about the other guy!*

It doesn't even matter that you know what's going on in the other person's life, as long as you understand that any mean or critical behavior comes from the other person's fear of being inadequate or rejected in some way! It's all about their need to feel better about themselves ... even though this is often so difficult to see or understand.

This information puts a new light on the dirty, mud-slinging campaigns often run by politicians, doesn't it? It tells us a lot about the self-concept of the mud-slinger!

I ask my students to fill out a "Deep Dark Secret Chart." It helps people apply the principles presented here and learn to look at the motivation beneath behavior, while not accepting the surface message that's being sent. Here is an example of the chart:

I always stress that we use the word *may*, as in "what *may* be their deep dark secret," because, since we're not God, we never know for sure!

It's important to clarify that some putdowns are intended to be fun. This is particularly common in middle school. It's entirely possible that a person is attempting to kid with you, but you may be particularly sensitive to the thing he is kidding about. You might be interpreting a tease as a putdown. That's why it's so important to pick an appropriate response; you don't want to attack a person who is just trying to have fun with you!

DEEP DARK SECRET CHART

Mean Behavior	Person wants you to believe	What may be their deep dark secret
Big brother hitting little sister.	He's strong, masculine, macho.	"I'm scared I'm not tough, I'm afraid I might be weak."
Teacher yelling at class for doing poorly on a test.	It's the kids' fault, they're lazy, irresponsible, don't care.	"I didn't teach this well enough; didn't know how to reach the students. I feel inadequate as a teacher."
Eighth graders acting stuck-up, being mean to other kids or ignoring them.	They're cool, popular, "happening," know what's going on.	"I have to act this way so no one sees what's really going on with me. I'm afraid I'm inadequate and have to act cool to convince people that I am."
Boss yells at his employees for not selling enough product.	It's the employees' fault; they should be working harder.	"I'm afraid that the product isn't good enough or that I'm not managing the business in an effective way."

COUNSELOR: Tracy, it's nice to see you in my office! What's going on with you? How's your life lately?

TRACY: Well, not so hot.

COUNSELOR: I'm sorry to hear that!

TRACY: Me, too.

COUNSELOR: What's happening?

TRACY: Well, everything was great for a while, then it all started falling apart. In fact, things *were* perfect!

COUNSELOR: Hmmmmm ...

TRACY: See, I have this new boyfriend. And he's the best. We have so much in common. We just clicked right off. And we spend a lot of time together. I've always wanted a steady boyfriend, I just never thought it would happen to me. He's the greatest!

COUNSELOR: Sounds great so far, but what's the problem?

TRACY: My friends! They've all turned on me! They won't even talk to me anymore.

COUNSELOR: I should have guessed. Do they have boyfriends?

TRACY: No, but they're nasty even when he isn't around. We used to all eat lunch together. Now, they won't let me eat with them, even though my boyfriend isn't there. They're always laughing and whispering when I come up to them, and one of them has been downright mean. She has made fun of my clothes, my make-up, my hair, she's even called my boyfriend a creep. She's getting all of my other friends to hate me.

COUNSELOR: Whew! That must be really painful! What are you thinking about doing?

TRACY: No idea! Nothing that I have tried has worked. That's why I came to you.

COUNSELOR: Well, I'm so glad you came in! And I do have some thoughts for you.

TRACY: Great. I need to do something. This has been killing me! My boyfriend says to just forget about them, but we've been friends for a long time. And even though I adore my boyfriend, I need my girlfriends, too!

COUNSELOR: I agree! Well, a big part of this might be to change your perspective about how you view this whole deal. Right now, I bet you're thinking there's something wrong with you and that's why they're rejecting you. But my guess is that you having a boyfriend has thrown your friendships all out of balance.

TRACY: You think so?

COUNSELOR: Yep, and here's what I mean. One year before I became a counselor, I got a teaching award. I found that my good and healthy friends were really happy for me. But I found that other members of the staff all of a sudden got critical, distant, and even mean with me! I didn't understand why this was happening, so I got some help from a wise friend.

TRACY: What did your friend say?

COUNSELOR: Well, he explained the whole concept of leveling. See, most people like to hang around with people whom they see at about the same level as themselves. That's where they feel comfortable. But let's say that a person decides that someone is "above" him. Maybe he decides the other person is prettier or smarter or more athletic. Or maybe he has just won an award he values, like in my case. Often that person feels inadequate around the guy who won the award. So he has two choices to try to get level again. He can change the way he sees himself, and decide that no one is really "above" him, that he is a good and adequate and lovable as he is. Or, he can try to find a way to "lower" the other guy. Which do you think most kids, and many adults, find easier to do?

TRACY: Lower the other guy?

COUNSELOR: Yep. Sad, but true. And what are some good ways to "lower" the other guy?

TRACY: Criticize him? Put him down?

COUNSELOR: Sure! That's what some of my fellow teachers were doing. Or another way, like in your case, would be for your friends to not invite you to do things with them. Turns out the real reason that my colleagues were being so unkind to me was that I'd received that teacher award. It had changed how they saw me. All of a sudden they viewed me as "above" them. That made them feel inadequate. And that's a way that most people don't like to feel. They didn't know what to say to themselves to feel better about their own teaching, so they tried to find ways to make me look bad.

TRACY: Well, this is sounding like my friends. But why would they see me as above them?

COUNSELOR: Well, it's hard to know for sure. But my guess is that the reason things have changed so drastically lately is because you have this cute new boyfriend.

TRACY: Oh, I never thought I was above them! I just feel lucky that he likes me. I'm not trying to be better than anyone.

COUNSELOR: They seem powerful. But I'm thinking that it's really a way of their dealing with the pain and jealousy they feel because they don't have boyfriends.

TRACY: I don't get why that works. Why does that make them feel better?

COUNSELOR: Well, if they can make you look or feel bad, it lowers your score and evens things out. Then they can feel that they are back to the same level as you. Then they don't feel so inadequate.

TRACY: That makes a lot of sense. But it's pretty sad, isn't it?

COUNSELOR: Yep. Remember that if they are doing unkind things to you, they can't feel great about themselves. And that's sad, too.

TRACY: Wow. I never thought that it might have to do with them! I feel bad that they are having such trouble dealing with my having a boyfriend. But I guess it's their job to handle that, and there isn't much I can do about how they respond to that.

COUNSELOR: Great thinking! Well, you can do your best to stay friendly, invite them to do things with you and give honest compliments to them when you can, because that could help raise their scores. This will be easiest to do when they aren't all together.

TRACY: Do you think that will help?

COUNSELOR: There's a good chance it will. I learned this from a friend I had in high school. She was uncommonly pretty and well dressed. Everyone tried to put her down, but somehow she figured out this whole leveling thing and made a real effort to be friendly and complimentary to all of us. That way, our score would go up, and we'd be at a level where we felt comfortable around her. When we got a compliment from her, because we valued her so much, it raised our "score!" There was no need anymore to criticize her.

TRACY: I could try that. I feel better just looking at this whole thing differently!

COUNSELOR: Yep, just changing your perspective on this should help you feel better.

TRACY: Thanks!

Translating

r. Wayne Dyer makes this wonderful assessment of human behavior in his book *Staying on the Path.*

"It isn't the world that makes you unhappy, or the way people are in the world. It's how you process the people and events of our world."

There is real power in understanding why people are critical of others, because then the recipient of the putdown or power struggle can *translate* what the other is really saying. The person being put down may not know exactly what is going on with the other guy, but at least he can translate to: "Hey, he's not doing too well right now! Wonder what's up with him?" It isn't important to know the root cause of the other guy's pain. It is important to know that for some reason he is not as loving to himself as he could be, and consequently, not loving to you. It is important not to judge or criticize the other person, because then you are committing the same error he is. *Compassion is the answer.* Just feel sad for him that he isn't doing too well at the moment.

I had a really pretty sophomore student named Amy who was dating a senior boy. The boy's former girlfriend enlisted the help of her friends, and they all started taunting Amy. Amy came to class in tears. In the hall, I spoke with her and ascertained what was going on. (This one wasn't too tough to figure out.) I asked Amy if she would be upset if she knew what they were *really* saying. I asked if it would hurt her feelings if this girl came up to her and said, "I'm really hurting because you're with my boyfriend and I'm not. I still like him, and I am also afraid that you might be prettier than I am. I am so weak that I have to get all my friends to help me put you down!" Once Amy started to translate what was going on, it no longer hurt her feelings! She could actually begin to feel some compassion for the jilted former girlfriend.

Here's another example. Let's say mom is yelling at her son, saying that he is lazy and irresponsible and that he needs to get his priorities straight. What if, rather than being hurt and defensive, the son translated his mom's outrage to this: "I'm not doing too well right now. I'm stressed at work, and I'm afraid I'm not doing a great job of parenting. I'm afraid you're not doing well because I'm not doing a good enough job as a mom, and I feel I have to blame you." The son could feel flattered that his mom loved him so much, and he could feel compassionate that she was fearful.

Or how about a teacher who yells at a class for being lazy and not studying and saying that's why they failed the test? An adept student could translate what the teacher was saying to this: "I'm afraid that I didn't teach you very well."

How about if a student walks into class and says, "What's up, you nerd?" The so-called nerd could translate that comment to mean, "Looks like he isn't doing too well today, not feeling too good about himself. Or maybe he's trying to impress someone. Or maybe he wants some power because he is feeling low on power right now and would like to see me act like an idiot so he can feel powerful. Well, no matter what the deal is, I feel sad for him. Think I'll blow this off and not let this hurt me at all!" Then, the "nerd" can pick from any number of appropriate responses explained later in the book. I got lots of practice translating in dealing with my former mother-in-law. Turns out that her frequent criticisms of me were really saying, "I miss my son, and I'm envious that you get to spend so much time with him."

If we don't learn to translate, we run the risk of taking the action or comment at face value. We then may allow it to damage our perception of ourselves. This is dangerous to our self-esteem. In the following quote, Dr. Wayne Dyer highlights why it is so vital that we not allow the comments of others to determine how we feel about ourselves:

"When you become immobilized by what anybody else thinks of you, what you are saying is that your opinion of me is more important than my opinion of myself."

It's true that it takes some ego strength not to believe what the other guy is saying. But the more people begin to think this way and respond appropriately, the stronger they will become. They will learn that they are handling what the world sends their way and feel proud that they can respond to difficult people and situations. It would sure help if all people were also receiving unconditional love and support from someone. But ultimately, *our self-esteem,* how we value ourselves, *is a choice we make in how to think about ourselves.*

This thought is well explained by Dr. Wayne Dyer in his book, *Staying on the Path:*

"You are always a valuable, worthwhile human being, not because anybody else says so, not because you're successful, not because you make a lot of money, but because you decide to know it."

Learn to look beneath the surface message that is being sent your way, and you will develop the ability to translate—a skill that could allow you to preserve your self-esteem while not getting entangled in an inappropriate or nasty interaction.

Examples of translation: (This is very similar to the "Deep Dark Secret Chart" except that in translating, we are actually changing the words the person is using to different words that will reflect the true, covert message, which will not be so painful.)

EXAMPLES OF TRANSLATION

Putdown	Possible Translation
"You're a loser."	"Something's going on with me right now."
"You're a geek."	"I'm not feeling great about myself right now."
"You think you're so cool!"	"I feel rejected that you aren't friendlier to me."
"Judy gets straight A's because she has no life!"	" You make me look bad. I'm afraid I'm stupid."

PARENT: Jimmy, you look sad. What's happening?

JIMMY: Nothing.

PARENT: Did something bad happen at school with a friend or the teacher, or is it something else?

JIMMY: Well, it's just this kid in my class.

PARENT: What's he doing?

JIMMY: Oh, I don't know.

PARENT: Is he being mean, or starting rumors, or leaving you out of things ... or?

JIMMY: Well, we got our spelling tests back today, and he said in front of everyone that I was the teacher's pet and that nobody liked me!

PARENT: Ouch! Whew, I bet that hurt!

JIMMY: Not really ... I just wanted to punch him.

PARENT: It's kind of weird that his comment didn't hurt you, because if someone had said that to me at your age, it would have really bothered me.

JIMMY: Well, I guess it kind of did ... but I still want to beat him up!

PARENT: Of course fighting is always an option. I hate to think about you getting all bloody and maybe having your face smashed in. I've always liked your face the way it is, but I guess in time I could get used to another configuration and I'd love you that way, too. But the neat thing is that there are a lot of other things to try before fighting.

JIMMY: Hmmmm ...

PARENT: Would you like to hear how I've learned to handle stuff like that?

JIMMY: Yeah, I guess ...

PARENT: We've already talked about how people only say mean stuff when they aren't feeling good about themselves, right?

JIMMY: Yeah ...

PARENT: Well, another thing I like to do is to "translate" what the other guy is saying. I try to figure out what the guy really means, and then remember his deep dark secret, not the words he actually used.

JIMMY: I don't follow exactly?

PARENT: Well, the kid in class said that you were the teacher's pet and that nobody liked you. But I bet he really meant something else.

JIMMY: Like what?

PARENT: Well, my guess is that his deep dark secret is that he isn't as good a student as you are. I bet he didn't do as well as you did on the spelling test. Is that true?

JIMMY: Yep. He's not very good at spelling. He's not too good at math, either.

PARENT: So, what if we *translated* what he said to what he probably was feeling ... his deep dark secret. What if he had said, "I'm not a very good speller and you are, and that makes me jealous of you! And I think the teacher likes you better, and that is hard for me, too." Would you want to beat him up if he said that, or would you feel sad for him?

JIMMY: I guess I'd feel sad.

PARENT: I would, too.

JIMMY: But it's hard to remember all that!

PARENT: Yeah, changing how we think about stuff takes some practice.

JIMMY: Well what if I can't figure out what he's really saying? You're old and smart.

PARENT: True! But if you can't figure out exactly what the whole situation is, you can always translate a nasty message to: *"I'm not doing too well right now, so I have to be mean to other kids."*

JIMMY: Okay.

PARENT: We don't have to know precisely what's going on with the other guy. We only need to know that if he isn't treating other people well, things aren't going well for him. So if someone says something unkind to you, how can you always translate his words?

JIMMY: "I'm not doing too well right now, so I have to be mean to other kids."

PARENT: Yep! Good memory.

JIMMY: Okay. Thanks. I think I can remember that.

PARENT: Now you know how to translate what he's saying. That's super. If you'd like to learn about some great things you can say back to him, just let me know. We can talk about that, too. Good luck!

How *Not* To Respond To Putdowns

It's important to remember what the putdown artist wants as a result of his bad behavior. Jim Fay asserts that the putdown artist sees it this way:

"I want you to act as small as I feel."

That will lower your score and raise his—bring your scores closer together—to make him more comfortable. Thus, any behavior that is immature, weak, unkind, or coming from fear will feed his need. He will make you look and act like an idiot, and consequently he will have met his goal to feel bigger, more powerful, or in control. The following are some behaviors that typically are immature, weak, unkind, fear-based, or self-defeating. These are ways to keep the bad guy after you:

1. Defending yourself, or becoming defensive, proving you're right (and the other guy is wrong)

EXAMPLES:
- "That's not true."
- "I never said that."
- "I am not a geek! Other people like me."
- "I am *not* fat!"
- "My other friends don't say things like that to me."
- "I do not wear too much make-up!"
- "I could too beat you up if I wanted to."

- "How can you say I'm a wimp? I won all-conference in track last season."
- "Son, I do not like her better; I treat you both the same!"
- "You just say that stuff because you're jealous!"
- "Well, if you hadn't left the cap off the toothpaste, maybe I'd feel like cooking a good dinner!"
- "If you students did your work, maybe I wouldn't be a boring teacher!"
- "If you didn't nag me, maybe I would call every night."

Gladys Moore, a counselor from the Denver area clarified why defending isn't a good idea:

"Making the other guy wrong doesn't make you right!"

In addition, the more you defend yourself, the more you add validity to the putdown. Confident people roll with the punches and realize that they don't have to prove anything to anyone. Plus, they know that it doesn't work.

2. Attacking back or retaliating verbally

EXAMPLES OF RETALIATING OR "GETTING INTO IT":
- "Well if you weren't so ugly, maybe you'd have some friends."
- "It takes one to know one!"
- "Butt-face!"
- "You can't make me!"
- "Oh yeah? Well, meet me after school. We'll prove who's tougher!"
- "Creep! Loser! Geek!"
- "So's your old man!"
- "Yeah, but I can always lose weight, and you'll always be ugly!"

- "#$@!!)))" (Using profanity.)
- "You're just jealous!"

> **"Profanity is the effort of a feeble brain to express itself forcibly."** **Unknown**

In a popular woman's magazine under the title, "Crucial Kid Comebacks to Use in Any Crisis," I found the following:

- "I know you are, but what am I?"
- "Oh yeah, you wanna make something of it?"
- "Go light a fart."
- "Yeah, but I can change, and you'll always look like that."
- "You're so immature."
- "That's so funny I forgot to laugh."

I was flabbergasted to discover that professional adults were actually recommending (albeit light-heartedly) these comebacks! Retaliating shows a lack of control and regression to childish behavior (even for children). It is therefore a weak way to respond. Handling the putdown in a feeble way is exactly what the other person is hoping for. It makes you look immature and like an idiot!

The definition in my dictionary for *taunting* reads: "To challenge or deride jeeringly." Note the use of the word *challenge*. Taunting is an invitation to "get into it." So, inherent in a taunt is the desire to get the other person to retaliate or to respond in a way that is going to meet the needs of the taunter.

Pointing out that the other person is using putdowns because he doesn't feel good about himself is a form of retaliation, which is not effective. It is true, and may cause the other person to do some thinking, but it will put the aggressor in the position of having to defend himself, and he will probably just attack the victim again.

EXAMPLE:

AGGRESSOR: "You're such a goon!"

VICTIM: "You're just saying that because you don't feel good about yourself right now."

AGGRESSOR: "What you are talking about? You're the goon here. Everyone knows that! I have friends. You're the one everyone hates!"

There are two wonderful *Far Side* cartoons that depict the classic futility of retaliation. In one, two guys named Al and Bob are stranded on a desert island. They are sitting on opposite sides of their only palm tree and obviously pouting. They have carved into the entire height of the tree: "Al's a moron. Bob's a jerk. Al's a moron. Bob's a jerk ..." In the other cartoon, a donkey and a rabbit are seated in a living room. The rabbit is saying, "Smart ass!" and the donkey is responding, "Dumb bunny!" It is clear that this conversation is going nowhere!

In America, putdowns have become something of an art form. I have learned this by presenting to a large conference of middle school students. When I ask them to generate some sample putdowns so that we can practice responses, I am overwhelmed with their repertoires and the cleverness of them.

SOME EXAMPLES:
- "You're so skinny, you could hula hoop through a Cheerio!"
- "You are so ugly that when you were born they slapped your mother!"
- "You have so few friends that they have to tie a pork chop around your neck so the dog will play with you!"
- "Did your mother have any children who lived?"

In one cartoon I saw in the newspaper, there was actually a "Creative Insult Competition." There was a panel of judges rating the putdowns on a ten point scale. They were holding up scorecards— 7.5, 8.2, 9.0—as the contestants were saying things like, "Bob, you have all the dependability of a public restroom soap dispenser!"

It's true that many kids interact by putting one another down for fun. If it's just play, that's great. However, it's frequent that these attempts to tease get misinterpreted (especially by the traditionally insecure adolescent.)

3. Telling the agressor that you're going to enlist help

This shows that you can't handle this problem yourself … it takes two or more of you to handle one of them!

EXAMPLES:
- "I'll get my big brother to take care of you!"
- "I'll get my friends to hate your friends."
- "I'll tell my dad. He'll take care of this."
- "I'll tell the teacher. You'll be in big trouble!"

There are conditions under which it is absolutely vital for a child to report harassment to the proper authorities. It's time to tell an adult if he feels that the child who is harassing him is "creepy" or "scary," that weapons may be involved, or that he is in true danger. If he has a strong sense or intuition that the situation in which he is involved is not safe, he must act to get help. It's important, too, to teach kids to trust their intuitions. He may say to his tormentor something like this: "I'm going to need to tell the principal about this. What's going on here is not okay."

If he says it in an adult, non-fear based, action-oriented way, it can be very effective. Tattling, or "telling" is immature behavior, so it will probably not be effective over the long haul. (For example, it may work on school grounds as long as the teacher or principal is around to protect the child, but what about after he leaves the school campus?) If he has not represented himself as strong and capable, the taunting is likely to continue. The child appears weak and dependent on others to solve his problems.

However, reporting a wrongdoing to the proper authorities in a calm and proactive way is a mature and even brave response. It takes a strong person to engage help when necessary, especially if it isn't a chronic response to the slightest transgression. Choice of words, tone of voice, and most importantly, the amount of fear beneath what is said will determine the effectiveness of the statement and action.

4. Using Sarcasm

EXAMPLES:
- "Oh, my heart is breaking...you're killing me!"
- "Well, thank you!" (said in a sarcastic tone)
- "You're a lot of fun to be around!"
- "I hope you don't think I'll take that seriously!"

Sarcasm is ineffective because it isn't honest. It's sneaky, indirect and manipulative. The person hearing it doesn't know immediately how to respond, because the true message is hidden. Strong people can be direct and honest. Someone once said,

"Sarcasm is a weapon of the weak."

5. Crying, whining, pouting, running away ...

or any other typically kindergartenish, childish or immature behavior. These responses readily show that the putdown has hit its mark!

6. Ignoring

There are occasions where ignoring mean behavior can work. Try it. If it works, great. Never change what works. But often, if the putdowns continue, a more effective tool is necessary.

7. Fighting, getting angry or violent

For years psychologists have recommended that people vent their anger into pillows and punching bags rather than pounding their loved ones. It's hard to argue that the former is more advantageous than the latter. However, researchers from Iowa State University have found recently that attempting to defuse anger by punching a wall or pillow is not effective. They conducted a study in which 700 students were deliberately made angry by insults and criticisms. The students were asked to spend two minutes either hitting a punching bag or sitting quietly. They then played a computer game that let them "punish" imaginary opponents with noise. Students who had whacked the punching bag blasted the noise louder and longer, regardless of whether they thought their imaginary enemy was the person who had insulted them originally.

The study summarizes that while violent actions may make you feel better at the time, they increase agitation in the long run. Why? Because instead of soothing yourself, you are feeding the anger, adding gasoline to the fire. The research found that it was more effective to take a time out, think things through and cool down.

I suggest that *it is profoundly more effective to change the way you view the criticism, releasing your fear of inadequacy and rejection.* Then, translate the other person's behavior to understand what it *really* means. Allow yourself to breathe deeply, take some time out, and choose a more peaceful and appropriate response. It's okay to take as much time as you need to do this. There is no need for an immediate response. Otherwise, as evidenced by this research, your anger may leave you feeling worse, not better. (All you have to say to the other guy at the time is, "I'll get back with you about this.")

In addition, I have often wondered if humans can't control their anger and get a handle on it, does that mean we have no control at all? Where does it stop? With murder? *Of course we have the ability to control our anger!* Otherwise, we would be totally out of control most of the time. The slightest transgression, insult or taunt would end in violence.

Charles Darwin wrote:

"The free expression by outward signs of an emotion intensifies it. On the other hand, the repression, as far as this is possible, of all outward signs softens our emotions. He who gives way to violent gestures will increase his rage; he who does not control the signs of fear will experience fear in a greater degree."

Harris and Klebold of the Columbine shooting are powerful examples of people who allowed their fear and anger to control them. There were so many other ways that they could have responded to the taunting they had experienced.

Harris and Klebold could have felt sad that the people who were picking on them were so unable to see their fine qualities. They could have understood the underlying weaknesses in the perpetrators of the insults delivered to them. They could have released their fear and said, "Oh well, you can't be liked by everyone!"

They made a deliberate choice to dress differently from the norm. Many of the taunts by their classmates were due to this. Harris and Klebold could have recognized on a conscious level that they were inviting a negative reaction. This was a choice they made. It was not, however, without consequences. They could have asked themselves why they were setting themselves up for this kind of harassment and decided whether it was worth it. Or, they even could have tried one of the responses explained later in the book and have regained their personal power non-violently.

8. Getting Revenge

Revenge is based on anger and fear. Clearly, revenge was a huge part of the motivation of Harris and Klebold in the Columbine killings. As they fired away, they shouted, *This is to all of you who made fun of us! Look who has the power now!* (Not an exact quote.)

This is an unevolved attitude, based on fear, and represents a low level of moral maturity and understanding. Some say that revenge is sweet, but I suggest that this is an immature, simplistic, unhealthy and fearful attitude. More advanced people suggest that the best revenge is living well. The negative repercussions of revenge are innumerable and obvious.

Problems with Revenge:

a. **Self-concepts are built and enhanced when people do brave, thoughtful acts, not cowardly, undisciplined ones.** If you respond to low, immature behavior with low and immature or even violent behavior yourself, it will lower your belief in yourself. People who do unkind things to others cannot have a strong, loving belief in themselves. This is an undeniable fact. Also, the other person has had enough power over you to cause you to behave in a reprehensible, cruel or mean way. He has made you look and act like an idiot, exactly what he hoped for.

b. **Hurting someone else does not help you deal with or understand the situation.** It does not help you heal, and it does not help you release your fear. It only creates more pain for both of you. It hurts not only the other person, but also yourself (for committing a cruel act and for not healing from the original insult). So, revenge triples the pain and may even incite more misery in the long run, if the other guy responds with more revenge.

c. **If all anger gets acted out with violence, where will it ever end? With everyone dead?** This is a fundamential way in which gangs operate. A trespass occurs, then a retaliation, then a feud is born, and the help of others is solicited. This can easily escalate into a small war. Remember Gandhi's great assertion:

An eye for an eye leaves everyone blind.

d. For all these reason, in the end, the **revenge can only be self-defeating.** Perhaps there is no more powerful example than Harris and Klebold of Columbine. They ended up dead. Even if they had not committed suicide, anyone can see that after their rampage, there were very few possible positive outcomes for their lives.

Usually the bully is more skilled at fighting and better prepared for battle than the victim of the putdown. You're entering his territory and playing the game on his terms. This is doomed to failure for the victim. Bullies are usually bigger than the people they pick on and good at fighting. That's why they do it. They are confident that they can win.

e. Revenge may cause violence. As evidenced by Harris and Klebold, and numerous other kids throughout the country, the revenge today may take the form of violence with devastating weapons. If those being taunted choose to retaliate, they often have to use weapons, as they know they can't win with their physical strength against the stronger bully. Today's avengers are packing scary instruments of mass murder, and as we have already witnessed, there is the potential for great harm. Both the perpetrators of the situation and innocent victims can be injured or killed.

f. Ultimately, what is the message about how we operate as a society? Do violence and revenge solve problems? Or do we believe that compassion, forgiveness, understanding and thoughtfulness are the best ways? If people are arming themselves to solve problems, what do young girls and boys do? What do you do when you have a knife, but the person assaulting you has a semi-automatic weapon? And what happens to the vital concept of learning to use our minds to solve problems? I believe that *the most powerful tool in the universe is a mind at peace.* No weapon can begin to match the power and effectivness of a mind that is functioning without fear.

When I started teaching at age 21, I had some 16-year-old boys in my class. I remember the day I tried to force a large ninth-grade boy to do something. He asked, "How are you going to make me?" I was furious and answered, "I have a boyfriend who has a black belt in karate." He laughed. We both knew that this was ridiculous. How was I going to get my boyfriend to drive across town to come to my defense when I needed him? It would have been so much better to have used my mind instead of the threat of violence. I needed to gain the skills to respond effectively to his resistive behavior without anger or aggression. Now that I know how to use my mind without fear and have gained a variety of skills for this type of situation, it seems ridiculous that I once desperately turned to this kind of threat.

I had a student named Michelle who told me an amazing story about revenge. Two weeks before the prom, her boyfriend broke up with her and asked another girl, Tracy, to the dance. Michelle was furious and very hurt. She interpreted this as the ultimate putdown. Michelle knew Tracy's younger sister and convinced the sister to allow her into Tracy's room on the day of the dance. Tracy had gone to get her hair done and had left her prom dress out on the bed in her room. Michelle sneaked into the room, snatched the dress and returned it to the store where Tracy had bought it, exchanging it for cash. Michelle then returned to Tracy's bedroom and left the money for the dress with a note that said, "You are NOT going to the prom with my boyfriend!" Michelle felt a deep satisfaction—for a little while. Then tremendous remorse hit her, and she confessed the story to me because she could no longer live with her guilt. It was killing her. She just couldn't believe that she could do something so mean to someone else.

The price tag of this revenge was huge. Needless to say, this act did not endear Michelle to her former boyfriend. It did not enhance her friendship with Tracy. It created a mess with Tracy's sister, who also suffered a great deal of guilt. But mainly, it destroyed Michelle's belief in herself. It turned out to be a humiliating and hurtful situation for everyone, but mostly for Michelle. The momentary satisfaction was outweighed tremendously by long-term guilt, misery, and damaged relationships. A more loving, empathetic and compassionate person would not have even experienced the original satisfaction

9. Portraying yourself as the victim

We are not in control of the majority of events or occurrences in the world. But we do have a tremendous power to use our minds. *We are in control of how we respond and react to situations.* When we act like victims, we are relinquishing that power and saying, in effect, "I am helpless here. You've taken my power. You've won." And then the other guy has won. But more importantly, you have given up the most valuable thing you possess: your power to use your mind in a way that feeds your belief in yourself and your ability to find joy.

10. Responding in other miscellaneous bad ways

There are millions of other responses loaded with fear and the need to make the other guy look bad. I've heard people say, "I'm not going to dignify that statement with an answer!" This isn't a terrible response. One could certainly do worse, but it's not my favorite, because it puts down the other person by implying that his comment was really awful. It's a form of retaliation that's nicely packaged.

A favorite line of elementary school students in response to being called a nerd or a geek is this: "I know you are, but what am I?" I'm not wild about it for the same reason as explained before. It's pretty nasty to the other person, and we don't want to stoop to his level. It is possible that this line could be effective, though, because it's a form of "outcrazying the crazies." (See Chapter 10.)

THE AFRAID/UNAFRAID PARADIGM

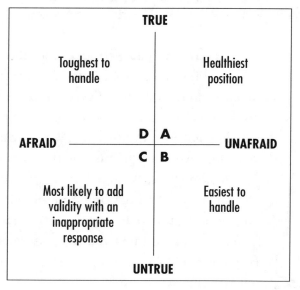

This chart shows the combination of factors possible when a putdown occurs. In Quadrant A, the putdown is true, but the recipient is neither afraid of being inadequate nor afraid of the other person's rejection of him on this issue. For example, I have seen elementary school kids criticize a young boy for having large ears. In fact, he did have large ears. The boy responded, "Yep, they're great for receiving radar transmissions! I can even sometimes communicate with other planets." The putdown was true, the recipient of it was unafraid about it, and the result was that he appeared very healthy. It isn't likely that the putdowns relating to his ears continued.

In Quadrant B, the putdown is untrue, and the person is unafraid. For example, if someone told you your skin was green, and you knew it wasn't, it would probably be very easy for you to laugh it off. This is the easiest situation.

In Quadrant C, the person being put down is afraid, but the putdown isn't true. I witness this a great deal with high school girls. Someone accuses them of promiscuous behavior. This is a false accusation, but they desperately want to preserve their reputation. So, they become defensive.

"That isn't true!" they say. "How dare you say that about me!" The more they protest and defend, the more true the accusation appears. Therefore, they add validity to the accusation with an inappropriate response, and inadvertently, they give power to the person doing the accusing. Young adolescents are extremely touchy about their sexuality. Perhaps the most powerful way to get to them is to accuse them of being gay, not because they are, but because they are so terrified that others might think they are. Of course, as they become more comfortable with their sexuality, gay or not, this accusation will not affect them so traumatically.

I can discover in which areas I still feel afraid, by recalling how I responded to situations in the past. If I found myself defensive or retaliatory, it was obvious to me that this was an area in which I still held fear. This is a subject where I am touchy. It's amazing how easily others seem to be able to find these touchy spots until we get a handle on them. They know how to find and push our buttons. Watch three-year-olds in the supermarket. They are experts at pushing the buttons of their moms! If, when others push our button, it "rings our bell," then we know that this is a topic where we are afraid. We need to gain some peace of mind.

The toughest situation to handle is Quadrant D, where the putdown is true and the person receiving it is afraid. For example, I have seen a big husky boy tell a smaller boy that he was a chicken and didn't want to fight him. True! The smaller boy did not want to fight the tougher kid because he knew what the outcome would be. Also, he was afraid of being inadequate in this area. Few boys like to admit that they are chicken.

A person who was less afraid would respond, "You're right! I don't want to fight you; you'd beat me up in a heart beat! Look at you, you're a mass of muscle! But I would like to be your friend ..." Who has the power now? Who looks healthier? Did the bully raise his score in this scenario? I have seen this kind of response work time and time again, but the key is that the person being put down must accept himself the way he is; even if he's fat, wimpy, chicken, skinny, smart ... or whatever! If he loves himself unconditionally and accepts that—even with his flaws—he is a valuable person, it will be very difficult to engage him in a power struggle. It will be difficult for the aggressor to gain what he's after: the ability to raise his score by making the other guy look or act like a fool.

It's interesting that many people know that a good offense makes the best defense. Many people will attack others first, before the other guys get to *them*. If I call you a nerd, who will guess that I really fear being one? I've noticed this when I play bridge. The best players sit back and admit their infrequent mistakes, while the players who are of questionable skill are the quickest to attack their partners. Their partners, fearful of being inadequate themselves, and scared that the criticism is true, are usually quick to engage in a battle to defend themselves and their play by criticizing their partner in retaliation. If they were confident in themselves and their talent, why would this be necessary?

Someone once expressed a similar thought:

"Name calling is the last resort of those who have no good argument for their position."

ADMINISTRATOR: Hi, Fred. You know I always like to see you! But I've heard the bad news from Mrs. Valdez that you've been in a fight.

FRED: Yeah, but they started it. And I just finally got sick of it!

ADMINISTRATOR: Sick of what, Fred? What's been occurring?

FRED: I've tried everything!

ADMINISTRATOR: I bet you have tried a lot of things! I know that you're a smart kid. So you've tried …

FRED: They've been picking on me and telling Mrs. Valdez that I've been swearing on the playground. I wasn't swearing, either! And they never let me play football with them at recess. And they called me fat!

ADMINISTRATOR: Well, that's a tough one. It doesn't feel good to be left out or criticized.

FRED: Nope, so I argued with them. I told them that I wasn't fat!

ADMINISTRATOR: What happened then, Fred?

FRED: They didn't listen at all. They just criticized me more. Then I tried to ignore them, but that didn't work, either. So I told them that they were mean, stupid creeps. I told them they were just jealous because I got good grades and they didn't. And I think Mrs. Valdez does like me better than them. I told them that!

ADMINISTRATOR: Mrs. Valdez said that there really might have been some swearing on your part when you tried this …

FRED: They made me really mad! I bet you'd swear, too.

ADMINISTRATOR: And then what did you do, Fred?

FRED: Well, one day, I couldn't help it.

ADMINISTRATOR: And so on that day you …

FRED: I started crying. It just got to me, and I couldn't help it. And I went to Mrs. Valdez. She was really nice and helpful. But later, whew, then I really got it! On the way home from school they threw rocks at me and called me a sissy and the teacher's pet. They said that only a true wimp goes and whines to the teacher.

ADMINISTRATOR: Sounds like this has really been traumatic for you, Fred. I can understand why.

FRED: So that night, when I got home, I talked to my dad. And he said that enough was enough. He said it was time for me to be a man and fight one of them. He said to wait until no one was looking, find one of them alone, and go ahead and hit him as hard as I could. He said that most boys have to do this at some point before they become men. He said that I had his permission. Then he and my mom started yelling at each other.

ADMINISTRATOR: Only problem here was that someone was looking, and you got caught, right, Fred?

FRED: Yeah, that, and I'm not a very good fighter. But he was!

ADMINISTRATOR: I'm not surprised to hear that. Usually kids who bully other kids are best at fighting, and not great at lots of other school kinds of things.

FRED: Yeah, well, I learned that.

ADMINISTRATOR: Well, the sad thing about all this, Fred, is that no matter who starts the fight, we have a rule in this school that both kids involved in the fight get suspended.

FRED: But that's not fair!

ADMINISTRATOR: Maybe not … but that's the way it works at this school. And it works that way in the real world, too. A dad named Bill got in a fight with another dad at a Little League game just recently. It was in all the papers. Bill really hurt the other dad, but he claimed that the other father started it. Guess what the judge said?

FRED: That it didn't matter who started it?

ADMINISTRATOR: Good thinking!

FRED: But I wanted to get even so bad!

ADMINISTRATOR: How did it work out?

FRED: Well, now I'm in more trouble than ever.

ADMINISTRATOR: Yep, and that's exactly what usually happens when people want to get revenge.

FRED: So what do I do now?

ADMINISTRATOR: Well, if you're open to trying some new stuff, how about coming in after your suspension is over, and I'll give you some thoughts on how you can handle this so it will work out better for you in the future.

FRED: Can't you just take care of them? Suspend them forever?

ADMINISTRATOR: I can see why you'd hope that I could do that! But it's kind of like the time you went to Mrs. Valdez. I bet she was very helpful, but what happened when she wasn't around?

FRED: They picked on me more.

ADMINISTRATOR: Exactly! So, I'd like to help you learn how you can solve these problems on your own. Do you think that this harassment occurs only here at Jefferson Elementary? Or, do you think it goes on in other places, too?

FRED: Other places?

ADMINISTRATOR: Yep, that's been my experience.

FRED: Oh …

ADMINISTRATOR: I care about you, so I don't want this kind of thing to keep happening to you. So, I'll look forward to talking to you when you get back, Fred.

FRED: Okay …

#2: JENNIFER, THE TEACHER AND THE FIGHT (QUADRANT D: AFRAID/UNAFRAID PARADIGM)

TEACHER: Okay, okay, girls, break it up!

STUDENTS: Argh …

TEACHER: Jennifer, when I walked up, you were straddled on top of Michelle pulling her hair. What started this?

JENNIFER: She said I had a B-52 nose!

MICHELLE: She does! We all call her Cyrano.

TEACHER: Michelle, I'll meet you at the assistant principal's office. Jennifer, I'd like to talk with you for a minute before we go down there …

JENNIFER: What?

TEACHER: Well, I'm just wondering, why did you let that fire you up so much? You really let her get to you.

JENNIFER: Yeah, well, you would too if you had a nose as big as mine!

TEACHER: Yeah, unless I weren't afraid to have a weakness or two … that's assuming that having a big nose is a weakness. Maybe it's an asset; did you ever think of that?

JENNIFER: What do you mean? At this school, kids hate kids who look different.

TEACHER: Well, I have pretty healthy thighs, and I've discovered that what I don't notice, or what I don't let bother me, other people don't seem to notice or be bothered by either!

JENNIFER: Not being bothered by having a big nose isn't as easy as it sounds ...

TEACHER: True, it's taken some effort on my part to change my thinking. But I've decided not to let the media, or society, or anyone else outside myself dictate my value as a person. I've decided to see myself as attractive and valuable regardless of what other people think. I value being healthy and active. But I've learned that not everyone can be model thin. And not everyone has a perfectly shaped nose. I think that noses that are a little different give people character. It makes them interesting!

JENNIFER: Hmmmm ...

TEACHER: I think you are a pretty neat kid, and I hate to see you lose belief in all the great things about you just because you don't think you measure up to a phony ideal that other people have established. Well, those are some things to think about. See you at the assistant principal's office.

JENNIFER: So what should I do next time when they say that?

TEACHER: Why don't you come by my room next week and I'll give you some things to try!

JENNIFER: Okay ...

#3: NICK, THE TEACHER AND THE DRUNK (QUADRANT B: AFRAID/UNAFRAID PARADIGM)

TEACHER: Whew! Nick, that was really exciting that we won the state basketball championship yesterday.

NICK: Yeah! Great. But you won't believe what happened. A dad from the other team came up to me after the game and challenged me to a fight. He said I was a wimp!

TEACHER: Wow, that's gutsy on his part. You're a wrestler, football player and track star. You're an amazing athlete!

NICK: Yeah, and he was drunk.

TEACHER: So what did you do?

NICK: Oh, I just blew it off. I didn't even pay him any attention. Guys like that just go outside and fall over in a ditch. I walked off and never saw him again.

TEACHER: Wow, I'm impressed with how well you handled that!

NICK: Thanks!

> *"What's important is not what others say to you, but what you say to yourself about it."*

Why Are You the
Victim of a Putdown?

I t's powerful to understand why putdowns or taunts might be happening to you. Here is a summary and review:

1. You may be interesting! Remember the tabloid syndrome. People talk and gossip about people they find interesting.

2. It may be because of leveling. You're too good! Someone is jealous. It's a back-handed compliment!

3. Something about you makes the putdown artist feel inadequate or rejected. You may have attracted the person he was in love with. He may think you set the police on his trail. He blames you somehow for his difficulties in life at the moment. You might cause these difficulties by being talented, attractive, or capable. In other words, as a result of your strengths and not because of anything you have done wrong, you are a threat to the other guy!

4. You might be in the middle of someone's bad day. It's random! You just happened to be in the lunch line when Mr. Negative dropped his milk.

5. The putdown artist needs power, control or attention, and you are just handy. Something about you might be different or unusual, but the deal still is that the other guy is not evolved enough to accept differences and be kind to all people. Or, on this particular day, he needs to use you to meet his power needs.

6. You're oversensitive. The other guy was just kidding, and you have a tendency to take things too personally.

7. It's possible that the putdown just slipped out wrong. I've done this a lot over the years. The words that came out of my mouth are not at all what I intended to say, and someone else might have taken offense.

8. You've responded in an inappropriate way in the past, and the putdown artist knows you are a good target. Using you is a super way for him to vent his aggression, because you respond in the way that he wants. You help make him feel powerful. It may be that you have refused to handle the situation yourself, relying on adults to "fight your battles." This will be perceived as weak by the aggressor and is likely to keep him after you. Some weak kids love to see lots of adults get all fired up as a result of their actions. The more people they get involved, the more powerful they can feel! The exception, as mentioned earlier, is in very serious situations, including those that involve weapons. In these cases, it's absolutely necessary to solicit the help of adults.

9. You might be choosing to do something that goes against the societal norm. This is certainly a choice you have. Understand, however, that in almost any society, one who chooses to go against the norm is likely to draw negative attention from the crowd. So, should you decide to dye your hair turquoise or wear a see-through plastic blouse, expect to hear strong reactions. Many courageous people have opted to go against society's rules and brave new frontiers. You might be one of these. But don't expect it to be without comments from the masses—many of them nasty. Ralph Waldo Emerson stated this concept beautifully:

> *"For your nonconformity,*
> *the world will whip you with*
> *its displeasure."*

10. You might be, through no choice of your own, different from others. You might be very tall, or fat, or you might have protruding ears. You might be a foreigner, have a speech impediment, or possess a limited mental capability. Your family might not have the financial advantages of your peers. It is tremendously sad that everyone hasn't learned to value all living humans, recognizing that we are all beautiful creations of God and inherently valuable. Those with maturity, compassion, self-love, and a spiritual orientation have learned to treat all humans with respect and dignity. Obviously, the person being critical of you has not yet achieved these levels.

TEACHER: Claudia, I overheard some kids making nasty comments to you today. That's really hard on my ears! I've told the other kids that, and they know that it's not a good idea to hassle my ears in the future. But I was wondering what your thoughts were on the whole deal.

CLAUDIA: I'm used to it. People at this school just want everyone to fit into their little preppy clique, and I'm just not like that!

TEACHER: : I follow you.

CLAUDIA: But I really hate them, and they have no right to make fun of my clothes.

TEACHER: Boy, I agree with you that it's a drag that they don't accept your clothes. But I'm wondering, what reaction did you think you'd get when you dyed your hair orange and purple and wore that floor-length, plastic zebra-striped coat?

CLAUDIA: Why can't people just accept me for who I am?

TEACHER: A great question. I've always wondered that, too. But it seems to me that since the beginning of time in organized societies, people have set fashion styles that they want the rest of the tribe to follow.

CLAUDIA: I think that's wrong. I think everyone should be free to be himself.

TEACHER: Probably so, but that doesn't change the reality of how it is. So I guess what I'm saying is that I agree that you have every right to wear what you want, as long as it doesn't disrupt the learning process in a big way. But I guess by now you know to expect that not everyone is going to embrace your decisions. If how you dress goes against the norm around here, you'll probably draw some caustic comments.

CLAUDIA: Yeah, well, I still think that's messed up.

TEACHER: Probably so. You say this doesn't bug you, and you're sounding like you don't want to do anything about it right now. If you ever change your mind, feel free to stop by and we can talk about some other options you have. Thanks for sharing your thoughts.

#2: MIKE, THE TEACHER, AND MIKE'S DAD

TEACHER: Mike, I heard something on the playground that really bothered me today. I heard other kids making fun of the fact that your dad passed away last year. That must be really hard on you.

MIKE: Nah, I just let it go.

TEACHER: Well, I'm glad it's not ripping you up, but if it were I, it would really bother me.

MIKE: It kind of does, sometimes, I guess. Why do they do that?

TEACHER: That's a great question, Mike. Lots of times people make fun of what they are afraid will happen to them. It's a sign that they are scared. See, they don't want to be different. And what do you think? Do you think that they think that they could handle losing their dads as well as you've coped with losing yours? Deep down, what do you think *they* think? Do you think they seem as brave as you are, or not as brave?

MIKE: Not as brave?

TEACHER: I agree. Not as brave at all! Seems like they haven't grown up as much as you have yet. And it's sad that because of what they are afraid of, they haven't learned to be more understanding of your situation. My guess, though, is that someday they'll learn and feel real badly about what they've said.

MIKE: So what do I do?

TEACHER: Well, I think an "I" message would be a really good thing to try. Want to stop by tomorrow and we'll work on one?

MIKE: I guess so. Thanks.

Great Attitudes for Responding in a Powerful Way

There are four great attitudes that will change the way you think and how you respond when faced with bullying tactics, putdowns or power struggles. And that change will help you de-victimize yourself, retain your relationships and maintain your belief in yourself. I've included many quotes here. Quotes help to serve as *memory hooks,* or ways to help people remember how to stay in the mode where they can say to themselves honestly, "Words will NEVER hurt me!"

1. Change your perspective. Hear what the person is really saying. The key to knowing how to respond to critical, nasty or mean behavior is to remember that it's about the other guy's need to feel better about himself. He might be saying, "I'm hurting right now," or, "I'm jealous of you," or "I need some power." In order for him to level the score, it must be that he sees you above him ... so you could even adopt the perspective that a putdown is a compliment!

It doesn't matter if you know exactly what's going on with the other person. Just trust that all negative behavior comes from negative feelings about oneself at the time of the behavior. *The putdown is a reflection of what's going on with the sender, not the receiver! It has to do with his needs to feel powerful, adequate, superior, or in control.*

In other words, *it's about the other guy* ... even if what he chooses to say may be true. It's vital to remember this, as Ken Keyes, Jr. points out:

"You make yourself and others suffer just as much when you take offense as when you give offense."

For example, I had to break up a fight between two girls one morning at my school. I asked them what started it. Mary said, "Rose said I had a fat ass, so I had to pound her!" The irony here was that Mary *did* have a rather extensive posterior. But Rose picked that because she knew it was a topic where it would be easy to "push Mary's button." In other words, Mary was afraid of being inadequate in this area. Rose was hoping to get Mary to *act as small as she* (Rose) *felt* ... which worked! But Rose wouldn't have started any of this if she had been having a great day. A healthy, strong Mary would have first realized that something was wrong with Rose that day. Then she would have acknowledged that we all have weaknesses, and that's okay ... yep, she had a rather large derrière ... and *that's* okay! Then, Mary would have responded in a way that would de-escalate the situation ... like, "I know, some people call it a double-wide!"

I heard about one boy who was teased for wearing thick, coke-bottle glasses in elementary school. At first he would get angry, but at some point in his young life he realized that the criticism had more to do with the criticizers than with him. He was then able to find his comic side. He'd pull his glasses out from his face so that his eyes grew huge! That tended to stop the tormentors.

Remember Jim Fay's wise advice:

"The idea is not to act as small as the other guy feels."

2. Release your fear of inadequacy and rejection. This means, don't buy in to what the person is saying! If he is any good at putdowns, he'll go for your jugular and try to hit a very sensitive area with you. After all, in order for him to feel better, it would really help if you acted like an idiot. Then he could say, "Look how powerful I am! I made that person who threatens me act like an idiot! Cool!" Here's where Mary made her mistake. See, she wasn't at peace with having a wide rear end.

Dr. Jim Keelan speaks to this issue in this poem from his book, *B.S.* and Live Longer (*Beat Stress)*:

If you could really accept
that you weren't okay
you could stop proving you
were okay.
If you could stop proving
that you were okay
you could get that it was okay
not to be okay.
If you could get that it was okay
not to be okay
You could get that you were okay
the way you are.
You're okay, get it?

I always tell my students and course participants:

"Never respond to fear with fear."

Carol Tavris writes in her book *Anger: The Misunderstood Emotion,*

"The key to managing a difficult person means first managing oneself."

Eleanor Roosevelt said:

"No one can make you feel inferior without your permission."

One of my favorite things to suggest to people is
"When your button is pushed, don't let it ring your bell."

The secret for not letting it ring your bell is to release your fear of being inadequate or rejected.

My friend's grandmother expressed this complex thought simply and memorably:

"When someone tells you to go to hell, you don't have to go!"

There is a great cartoon from *Peanuts* where Lucy is attacking Linus. She's yelling, criticizing him, and raising a big fuss. Linus is saying nothing. Charlie Brown approaches and asks, "Are you two fighting?" Linus answers, "She's fighting; I'm just sitting here!"

Cyrus Ching adds support for not engaging in the power struggle:

"I learned long ago. Never wrestle with a pig. You get dirty, and the pig loves it!"

3. Do not defend and prove! This never works. As mentioned before, it only gives power to the offender and actually *adds* validity to their assertion. You do not want to be in a defensive stance. Your most powerful and healthy position is one where you do not try to make the other person wrong.

4. Use techniques that make you a poor future target. Learning some skills that you can use in these situations can have a huge payoff. These skills will de-escalate the situation immediately, preserve your self-concept, and almost always cause the bully to look for another target. If you do not respond in a way that gives him more power, he's very likely to go look for someone who will. These techniques have a variety of applications, and their use depends on your personality and the nature of the situation.

I had a student last year who told me the story of his experience in a special class for gifted kids, called "s" class. The students who weren't selected for the special program began making fun of the gifted kids, calling them nerds and geeks. The gifted kids felt hurt, believed the unkind words, and withdrew to themselves.

They made friends among themselves, and as time went on, they developed a much stronger belief in themselves. They learned to have fun together, and they changed their perspective about the other students. They started to feel sad for them, they began to see that the other kids were jealous and felt insecure. The gifted kids didn't respond to the negative comments, choosing not to "wrestle with the pigs." They chose to not allow anyone else to make them feel inferior. They retained their dignity, and had a great time at school. The healthiness of the gifted kids was undeniable, because they chose to respond to the putdowns, and life in general, in a positive way. (In the next chapters, I will describe some of the responses they used.)

The other kids started to see what fun the "s" class was having and felt left out. The strength of the gifted kids was appealing, too. Eventually the putdown artists wanted to join the kids they had previously called "nerds." The "s" class kids again showed their healthiness by allowing these friendships to develop, choosing not to carry grudges. In the end they all became friends and remained friends for years. This is a wonderful model of what can happen when people change their perspective of a situation and release their fears.

Even if you employ a super comeback, one that is recommended in this book, do not expect that it will always work immediately on everyone. Sometimes, if you don't respond as the perpetrator hoped, it will make him feel even more inadequate and powerless, and anger might be the result. That's okay! Understand that his anger is a reflection of his inability to get you to respond as he had hoped. Don't let his anger control you. Say to yourself something like, "Wow, look at the veins pop out on his face! He's really getting red, too! He really can't stand that I'm not letting him push my button. How sad for him." Then walk away, congratulating yourself on not engaging.

Some people—very few, in my opinion—really are incorrigible bullies who lack a conscience. They need serious therapy or institutionalization. If you try everything suggested here and nothing works, seek the help of a professional.

Often, it just takes a while for the person to learn that you are not going to respond as he had wanted. Stick to your guns! In time, the person will learn that you are not a good target for his lowly tricks. I've had students who consistently try to involve me in a power struggle. They remain persistent, because this particular tactic has probably proved beneficial for them in the past with someone: a parent, another teacher, or a classmate. They say things like, "You can't make me do this!" I answer, "True! If you'd like credit, however, it's due in twenty minutes." Gradually a new pattern of interaction is established, and they learn that I am not going to play their game.

TEACHER: Michelle, it's great to see that you've come by.

MICHELLE: Well, I gave some thought to what you were saying in class the other day, and I'd like to have some ideas about what else I can do when people make fun of me. Being nasty and sarcastic just doesn't feel very good to me.

TEACHER: I know what you mean. It doesn't feel good to be nasty to people. I'm glad to help. I see it as a four-step process. First, it's helpful to change your perspective.

MICHELLE: Oh yeah, I remember. We talked about that in class. It's really about the other guy. They're not doing so well at the time if they say something mean to me. I forget about that sometimes.

TEACHER: Yep, it's easy to forget, especially when they strike on something we're sensitive about. And that's what people normally do. They know which areas to attack. I bet if you wanted to make your mom mad, you'd know just what to say.

MICHELLE: That's true!

TEACHER: So you've got the first step. Change your perspective. It takes a little practice to remember to always do this, but I bet if you work on it, it will become pretty automatic. Then, the other day, we talked about the next thing to do. Release your fear of being inadequate or rejected. Here's what I mean. It's okay if not everyone loves you. It's okay to have flaws or things that are different from others. It must be, because we all do. We all make mistakes. We all have weaknesses. That's how we all got created. Once we accept that, we've got it made!

MICHELLE: I guess that's true.

TEACHER: And you'll notice, that the people who seem to have the most friends are the ones who worry the least about always being accepted by everyone. So, the idea is, when someone pushes your button, don't let it ring your bell.

MICHELLE: That's easier said than done.

TEACHER: With a little practice, it gets easier each time. It's just a matter of breaking a habit and taking a risk to try something new.

MICHELLE: Mmmmm ...

TEACHER: Then, third, don't get defensive. It's not effective. Don't try to prove that you really don't have flaws or that what they are saying is wrong.

MICHELLE: I know, it never works! I try to prove that I'm right to my mom, but it never gets me anywhere!

TEACHER: Yup, I just don't know many people who say, "Oh, I guess you're right! I was thinking that your thighs were big, but now that you point out that they aren't, I agree with you!"

MICHELLE: So what do I say?

TEACHER: Well, the fourth step is to use effective techniques, like "I" messages, neutral responses, negative assertion, outcrazy the crazies, and more. Would you like to learn those?

MICHELLE: Sounds better than what I've been doing.

TEACHER: Great ... come by anytime.

"I" MESSAGES

Thomas A. Gordon wrote about "I" messages in his books, *Parent Effectiveness Training* and *Teacher Effectiveness Training*. The main idea of an "I" message is to confess to a feeling, weakness or problem. The reason they are so effective in responding to putdowns is that it takes a healthy person to admit a feeling, weakness or problem. If you respond to a putdown in a *healthy* or *mature* way, you are raising your score, thereby *increasing* the difference between your score and that of the person doing the criticism. This is exactly what you want to achieve, as it makes the other person even more uncomfortable when thinking about using putdowns on you. What he wants is for you to act in a small, immature way so that your scores become closer, not farther apart.

In addition, most people don't respond well when they are told what's wrong with *them* or what they should do. These comments often take the form of "you" messages. For example: "You spend too much time on the phone!" Most people respond in a defensive or attacking way, saying, "I do not!" OR, "If you had any friends, maybe you'd spend some time on the phone, too!" However, if the person were to say, "I need to use the phone soon," most people would respond with, "Okay! No problem!"

I learned about the powerful difference between "I" messages and "you" messages when a group of friends and I were trying to find our seats at a Denver University hockey game. The game had already started, and we had to walk in front of people to get to our seats. One person yelled, "Down in front!" (This was a "you" message, since commands have the understood subject of "you.") All of us got a little defensive, since we were doing our best to be seated. One person in the group even responded with something nasty, as I recall. As we forged ahead, someone else said, "I can't see!" (a clear "I" message), and all of us immediately ducked down and continued walking in a crouched fashion; someone in our group even apologized.

Why did we respond this way? Because we really didn't want to block anyone's view, but like most normal Americans, we didn't like being told what to do!

It seems that the difference is small, just a choice of words. But the resulting difference in the message is powerful. Actually, the entire message is changed from "There's something wrong with you," or "I need to tell you what to do," to "I have a problem that I need your help with." That is a very strong implied message to send to people, and most will respond favorably, because most people want others to know that they care about their feelings.

Another vivid example of the power of "I" messages occurred when I was teaching eighth graders about putdowns and "I" messages. I had explained all the basic concepts and then suggested to my class: "Get out there and get put down so you can try some of these new skills!" A baffled girl returned to me after the next class. She told me this story. It seems that when she arrived in her typing class, a boy next to her said, "Hello, bitch." She was all prepared to respond to putdowns on this day, so she answered, "Ooh, I need to let you know! That really hurts my feelings!" The boy answered immediately, "Oh, I'm sorry!" She returned to my room perplexed and asked, "If he was so remorseful, why did he say that in the first place?" This can be a tough one for kids (or adults, for that matter) to understand. Why did he say that mean thing in the first place? Who knows? Maybe he felt like Cletis that day. Maybe he wanted to try out the word. Maybe he liked her and thought that swearing would impress her (sometimes the workings of the adolescent mind can be truly perplexing).

But the point is, he said it because somehow it filled his needs; *he didn't say it to hurt her!* When confronted with the fact that it did hurt her, he felt bad.

Remember the words of American author and journalist Gene Fowler:

"Men are not against you; they are merely for themselves."

In other words, they are doing what they are doing in order to *meet their own needs, whatever they may be, not really to hurt you.*

I'll admit, sometimes this is difficult to understand or to apply to some situations, because it truly appears that the person wants to hurt the other. And there are some people who truly defy all techniques or approaches. But "I" messages will be effective eventually with most people if done correctly. I just recommend that you try them and see how powerful this admission of vulnerability can be.

Again, the reason that being vulnerable can often be a powerful stance is that it takes a very healthy, strong person to be able to admit weaknesses and express feelings. It sends the implied message, "I trust you not to hurt me, now that you know how you can." It is usually well received.

I noticed another example of this concept while observing two waitresses at a restaurant.

One patron asked, "Where's my coffee?" The first waitress answered, "You didn't order any coffee!" (Remaining in a power position.) The person responded angrily, "Yes I did, and I want it immediately!"

In the second situation, a woman asked, "Where's the coffee I ordered?" Waitress number two responded, "Oh, I'm sorry! I totally forgot!" (Admitting a weakness.) The patron responded, "Oh, that's okay; bring it when you have a chance."

Shakti Gawain states in her book, *Creating True Prosperity:*

"In our society, power is generally honored and respected, while vulnerability is judged as weak, embarrassing, and shameful. Because of this cultural bias, most of us attempt to develop our power in one way or another and eradicate, or at least hide, our vulnerability. This is especially true for men because the traditional bias against vulnerability in men is enormous. The problem with this stance is that as humans we simply are vulnerable. Trying to overcome this fact will not make it go away. At best, we learn to hide it from ourselves and others, which leaves us living in denial. Even sadder, we are attempting to rid ourselves of an essential ingredient to a satisfying life. Our vulnerability is the doorway to our receptivity; without it we cannot receive love, we cannot experience intimacy, we cannot find fulfillment."

SO WHAT EXACTLY ARE "I" MESSAGES?

There are many differing opinions on the "I" message form; here are several key components.

1. You do everything possible to avoid the word *you*, even the "understood you" (as in a command).
2. You disclose a feeling that you actually experience, or a problem that you actually have. It is vital to be honest; otherwise, these can be viewed as extremely manipulative.
3. You do not use an angry tone of voice or body posture.
4. Your intention is *not* to tell the other people what is wrong with *them* or what *they* need to do, but rather to reveal how *you* respond to a certain situation.

Jim Fay clarified the purpose of "I" messages this way:

"The real reason to use an 'I' message is to achieve very clear, honest communication without attacking the receiver or creating additional problems for the sender."

SAMPLE #1:

I feel_____(describe feeling) when
_____ (description of what has happened in the passive voice or avoiding the use of the word you if possible) and then I _____ (reaction to this situation, based on the value system of the person to whom the "I" message is being delivered.)

EXAMPLE OF #1:

As a mom, you are reacting to finding the kitchen chores not completed by your loving offspring:

"I feel really bummed out, or overloaded, or upset, etc. (feeling) when I come home and find that the kitchen is a mess and the dishwasher isn't unloaded (what has happened) and then I want to retreat to my bedroom and read a book instead of cooking dinner." (reaction, based on the value system of the kids=eating).

SAMPLE #2

I feel_____when_____and when
I feel_____(repeat #1), I _____(reaction).

EXAMPLE #2:

I feel really exasperated when I come home and the kitchen is a mess, and when I feel exasperated, I want to escape to my bedroom to read instead of cooking.

SAMPLE #3

When _____(description of what has happened)
I get _____(feeling) and then I _____(reaction.)

EXAMPLE #3:

When I get home and the kitchen is a mess, I get really bummed out and then I don't feel like cooking at all; I want to go to my bedroom to read.

THE THREE PART "I" MESSAGE

It is important that the feeling word is as strong as possible while still being true. For example, many people say they feel "uncomfortable when ..." This is not a real attention grabber. The feeling word should fit the person using it, too. Football players *can* use "I" messages ... they just need to pick feeling words that fit them. Instead of saying they feel "distraught," they might say "really bummed out"— or use some expression that better fits their style and personality.

Sometimes, it's hard to leave the *you* out of the second part. But the idea is that it's not exactly *you* causing this reaction in me, *it's the situation!* In other words, anyone who did this particular thing would cause the same reaction in me. It's about how *I* handle things.

For example, I told my husband once, "You're driving too fast." *("you" message)* His response was, "No, I'm not; you're riding too slowly." *(defensive)* I discovered later that it really was *my* problem. He was happy driving that fast; *I* was the one who was uncomfortable. Perfect time for an "I" message!

PART I: DESCRIBE THE FEELING AS STRONGLY AS POSSIBLE

"Honey, I feel uncomfortable ...

Nope! The word "uncomfortable" is too weak.

"Honey, I get scared to death.

Much better, and it's true.

PART II: DESCRIPTION OF WHAT HAS HAPPENED IN THE PASSIVE VOICE OR WITHOUT A "YOU"

When you drive this fast ..."

Nope! This still makes him wrong. There's a "you" in there!

When I'm in cars going over 70 miles an hour ..."

Better. It's not your driving. It's the speed that causes my fear, regardless of who is driving.

PART III: REACTION, BASED ON THE VALUE SYSTEM OF THE OTHER PERSON.

... and then I get really mad."

Nope! This is not into his value system! Many people get a kick out of making others mad, especially passive aggressive people.

"and then I don't even want to be in the car."

Better choice. It is into his value system! If he's my husband and cares about me, he should want me to be in the car with him.

An alternative "I" message: *"Honey, I get scared to death when I'm in cars going over 70 miles an hour, and then I don't even want to be in the car."*

His response: "Women!" And he slowed down.

EXAMPLES OF POTENTIALLY EFFECTIVE "I" MESSAGES

Child to his mother who yells at him to do his homework

"Mom, I feel devastated when I am yelled at to do my homework; then I go upstairs and can't even concentrate."

Child to another child

"I feel really hurt and left out when people whisper and exclude me from the conversation, and then I don't even want to be around them or be their friend."

Overweight person to someone who has criticized his weight

"I feel persecuted when people criticize my weight, and when I feel that way, the weird thing is that I often go home and eat!"

Teenager who gets criticized frequently by parents

"When I get criticized a lot, I get so depressed that I don't even want to stay around the house. I feel like leaving and being with my friends."

Big brother to a little sister

"I feel frustrated when I am interrupted when I'm trying to do my homework, and then I don't feel like spending time with you or taking you for an ice cream." Later: "Hey, just wanted to let you know, it's great when I can get my homework done without being interrupted, and then I feel like taking you somewhere fun!" This is classical Skinnerian "shaping of behavior" using reward and extinction. This approach would probably be tremendously effective with a younger sibling, especially if "Big Bro" takes her for ice cream!

Secretary to an angry parent on the phone

"I get so unsettled when I hear swearing on the phone that I can't even concentrate on what's being said or how to solve the problem."

THINGS TO REMEMBER ABOUT "I" MESSAGES

- All three parts are not always necessary, especially with playground putdowns.
- They must be true.
- They tell people how their behavior is affecting you, and give them a choice about the inevitable consequence.

For example, the mother in sample #1 is letting her kids know that if they want her to cook, they must complete their kitchen chores. They have a choice about this matter. And so does she! The mom is not telling them what to do but rather how she will respond to what they do. This is wonderful because it empowers the children to make a good choice, and she can enforce it. She cannot make them clean the kitchen, but she can choose not to cook. I could not make my husband drive more slowly, but I could choose not to get in the car with him the next time.

As a teacher, I often use three-part "I" messages. Here's an example:

"I get frustrated when students don't listen to what I say in class, and then I feel like giving pop quizzes or more homework." (Clearly, pop tests and homework fit into their value systems.)

I've often heard teachers use an ineffective third part:

"I get frustrated when students don't listen to what I say in class, and then I get really mad and take it out on my husband!" (Many students delight in making the teacher angry ... even in making her cry! What happens when she gets home is totally irrelevant to them. But they wouldn't be interested in frustrating the teacher if they knew it meant extra homework for them!)

POSITIVE "I" MESSAGES

"I" messages can be effective when delivering a positive intention. I like to say in class:

EFFECTIVE:

"I get really excited when I see everyone working hard and learning, and then I feel like bringing cookies on Friday, or lightening up on homework over the weekend!"

INEFFECTIVE:

"I get really excited when I see everyone working hard and learning, and then I feel like going out to dinner and a movie with my friends this weekend!"

Both statements are true, but which one grabs the attention of the students?

WAYS TO "MESS UP" "I" MESSAGES

- Use anger or sarcasm in your tone of voice.
- Use controlling or angry body language.
- Sound like you're telling the other person what's wrong with them or what they should do, as opposed to telling them what problem *you* have.
- Deliver them to more than one person at a time (These are best when delivered one-on-one, eyeball-to-eyeball. If, for example, a student is being hassled by a group of other students, it will *not* be effective for the hassled student to address the whole group at once. He needs to select the kindest, most approachable of the lot, find a time when the two of them can be alone or with a facilitating adult, and deliver his "I" message at that time.) The reason it usually isn't effective to send an "I" message to a group is that there can be much more support for immoral or inappropriate behavior in a group,

whereas an individual is often forced to confront his conscience and his guilt.

- Use one in the middle of a heated argument (they work best when both people are calm and the problem situation is *not* occurring). Wait for a calm moment or set an appointment. Tell the other person that you want to talk about something you've noticed about yourself.

SOME MYTHS ASSOCIATED WITH "I" MESSAGES

Jim Fay taught me that there are many misunderstandings associated with "I" messages. I'd like to clarify some of them.

1. "I" messages make other people do things.

TRUTH: "I" messages can help the sender feel dignified, less threatened and less put down. There is always a choice for the receiver. He might choose not to care about your feelings or to accept the consequences you have described.

2. If "I" messages are done correctly, they'll work.

TRUTH: There are no guarantees; however, they should raise the odds.

3. "I" messages are the only correct way to confront a problem.

TRUTH: They are an additional tool in our repertoire for dealing with people.

TRUTH: They can even make "you" messages more powerful. If a person is careful to use "I" messages and saves a "you" message for a critical or dangerous situation, the "you" message packs more punch. In my classroom, I save "you" messages for emergencies or when I want the attention of my students in a hurry. For example, I'll say, "Quick! Sit down!" Since this is a very unusual way for me to treat them, they pay attention. This can be very important when a child is heading toward a power line. If, however, he hears commands all the time, the child will have a tendency to tune them out.

TRUTH: They are probably best for situations in which both the issue and the relationship with the other person are very important. For example, it's probably never appropriate to use an "I" message when someone cuts you off in traffic. Your relationship with the person isn't that important. Imagine how awkward it would be for you to say, "I feel terribly hurt when cars cut me off ..." That's why "I" messages are best used for friends, family, mates, co-workers, and in situations that are important to you.

4. It's necessary to use all three parts of the "I" message.

TRUTH: Sometimes the third part doesn't fit. Sometimes just the first two parts are adequate, or often, just the first part alone will do the trick. It's best for the sender to use his judgment in the situation. The one part form of "I" message is particularly helpful to students when responding to putdowns, as it is difficult to generate a three-part "I" message on the spot. Here are some examples of using just the first part of the "I" message.

- *"Ooh, that hurts!"*
- *"Wow ... that scared me!"*
- *"I'm pretty bummed about this!"*
- *"Man, that was painful to me."*
- *"Wow, I'm not handling that well at all."*
- *"I'm getting really frustrated (bummed out, hurt, or sad)."*
- *"Gee, this is exciting to me!" (Positive "I" message.)*

5. A good communicator can always think of an effective "I" message on the spur of the moment.

TRUTH: "I" messages often demand a great deal of thought and even practice in some instances. I have worked with students on writing an "I" message, asked them to practice it, then wait until an appropriate time to deliver it. Often several days pass throughout this process.

6. "I" messages will always bring immediate results.

TRUTH: The value of an "I" message is often reduced by insisting on an immediate response.

Once I delivered an "I" message to my mother-in-law. She had been critical of my father, and it really bothered me. I told her that it hurt me deeply when people criticized my father, and then I usually took out my pain on my husband (her son) by being crabby and unreasonable. She responded by saying, "Well, I don't care about your feelings." Whew! I wasn't expecting that one. But about two months later, I started getting potholders in the mail from her. Turns out she did honestly care about my feelings. She just felt guilty about her inappropriate comment and was taken aback that someone would call her on her bad behavior. By the way, she probably would have felt less guilty if I had been able to tell her this alone and not in front of her son.

7. "I" messages can be used in any situation.

TRUTH: "I" messages can be very embarrassing or ineffective when delivered to a person in front of other people. For example, if I said to a student in front of the entire class, "That last comment really hurt me," he would probably have to respond with something nasty in order to save face. If I asked him to go in the hall and told him one-on-one, his reaction would probably be to apologize.

Again, this is important information for students who are dealing with a group of kids who are putting them down. An "I" message to the whole group will probably be ineffective, since the group is just too powerful for one person to confront. But face-to-face with one member of the group, an "I" message can be very effective, since the person doing the criticizing is not really trying to hurt the other person but trying to meet his own needs. In addition, he will be forced to deal with his own guilt and conscience.

8. "I" messages work with all people.

TRUTH: "I" messages are not effective with psychopaths, or those who have no conscience. Don't dream of trying one with the likes of Ted Bundy, Charles Manson or Hitler. Fortunately, psychopaths represent a very small percentage of the population. It can sometimes be difficult to use an "I" message with a person who has power over you, like a boss or parent. I suggest you give it a try; it will tell you a lot about the compassion level of the person in power.

WHY DON'T WE HEAR "I" MESSAGES MORE OFTEN?

I have found that it is very difficult to teach students to use "I" messages. I think this is for a variety of reasons.

1. Students rarely hear adults use "I" messages. In movies and on television, heroes generally go after their enemies to prove who's boss. They break chairs over their heads, hold them at knife point, shoot them with semi-automatic weapons, construct massive plots of revenge, and blow up cities to get even.

2. They are afraid to make themselves vulnerable and don't understand the positive power of "I" messages.

3. They may not know how to respond to the other person's response. What do I say if the other guy responds in a negative way to my "I" message? Sometimes, an "I" message can catch a person feeling guilty about what he just said, and his response to your "I" message might not be the love-filled apology that you expect. It's a good idea to be armed with a second response. We can thank Jim Fay for many of these wonderful retorts.

If he says, *"I don't care about your feelings."*

You can answer: *"Oh, I had you figured wrong! I thought you were the kind of person who cared about others' feelings."*

Or: *"That's good information for me."*

Or: *"Sorry to hear that!"*

If he says, *"You shouldn't feel that way."*

You can answer: *"I know, I probably shouldn't, and I do."*

Or: *"I know, I'm still working on this one, but I haven't conquered it yet."*

Or: *"Were you thinking I should feel like you do?"*

If he says, *"Good, I was trying to hurt you.."*

You can answer: *"Oh, I had you figured wrong ... "*

Or: *"Sorry to hear that."*

Or: *"Sorry to hear that, because I was hoping we could be friends."*

If he says, *"I'm just telling you the truth, trying to help you."*

You can answer: *"Thanks for your thoughts."*

Or: *"Interesting to know how you see it."*

Or: *"Yes, and it's hurtful to me that you feel that way."*

WHEN IS THE BEST TIME TO USE "I" MESSAGES?

The best occasion for an "I" message is when the issue and the person involved are both important. Often, the putdown issued is a real "zinger" or one that hits in an area where you are very sensitive, like your race, family, or profession. Of course, if you were totally unafraid of being inadequate, you wouldn't be sensitive in these areas. But, since we are human and have tender areas, "I" messages are great for those occasions. "I" messages are time- and effort-consuming to generate and thus should be used only for the special people and important situations in your life. Do not waste these powerful messages on passing people and issues. Again, imagine how ridiculous it would sound if, after a car cut you off in traffic, you said, "I feel hurt and abused when I get ignored in traffic, and then I feel like slowing down and causing cars to pile up behind me."

TEACHER: Mike, we talked the other day about kids making fun of you because your dad died last year. You said that you might be interested in learning about a technique that could work to stop these kids from saying such hurtful things. Are you still interested?

MIKE: Kind of interested.

TEACHER: Well, I already know that you are a brave kid because of how well you're handling living without your dad. This technique takes a pretty brave kid, so we've got the right guy here.

MIKE: I guess ...

TEACHER: This may sound a little weird at first, but here's what I'm thinking you could try. Let's say a bunch of kids say something about your dad. Pick the nicest kid in the group, and try to find a time later when you can talk to him alone. Then just tell him that it really hurts you to hear people talk about your dad being gone.

MIKE: I don't want to tell them that they hurt me. I'm a guy. They'll make fun of me!

TEACHER: I can see why you'd think that, Mike. But here's my question for you. Which takes more guts, admitting a feeling or pretending that it doesn't exist?

MIKE: Admitting it?

TEACHER: Good thinking. So see, when you admit a weakness or a feeling, you actually appear *stronger!*

MIKE: I don't know about this ...

TEACHER: You know what else makes this tough, Mike?

MIKE: Not exactly ... I can just tell that the thought of it feels weird in my stomach.

TEACHER: Well, you probably haven't heard a lot of people do this.

MIKE: I've heard you talk about your feelings sometimes ...

TEACHER: And do you remember how it worked?

MIKE: Not exactly ...

TEACHER: One day, I was coming back from lunch, and one of my students said I looked like I was waddling. That really hurt my feelings. So I told him that. Do you know what he said?

MIKE: Nope.

TEACHER: He apologized right away! He said he was just kidding, he didn't mean to hurt my feelings. See, my guess is that these kids don't really want to hurt *you;* my guess is that they just want to feel better about themselves and what they are afraid of.

MIKE: What a weird way to do it!

TEACHER: Isn't it? You said that these guys were pretty important to you, didn't you?

MIKE: Yeah ...

TEACHER: Good, because you wouldn't want to use up all this effort on kids who weren't important to you or on a situation that didn't matter.

MIKE: Okay.

TEACHER: So, do you think you're interested in giving this a try, or would you like to hear about something else?

MIKE: I'm pretty sure I'm ready to go for it.

TEACHER: So, there are a few things to remember. First, make sure you start with "I" ... like, "I get really hurt when I hear people say stuff about my dad." This won't work if you start with "you" ... like, "*You* guys better quit talking about my dad!" So what do you say?

MIKE: I say, "I get hurt when I hear people say stuff about my dad ..."

TEACHER: Exactly! And how many people do you tell this to?

MIKE: One at a time?

TEACHER: Yep! And should you say it in an angry voice or a nice, soft and calm one?

MIKE: Soft and calm?

TEACHER: You got it. Do you think it will work right away?

MIKE: Maybe not?

TEACHER: Right! But I bet in time you'll find that it just isn't any fun anymore for these guys to say stuff like this to you. You're just too strong, and they will feel guilty and bad. But it may take some time for this to sink in for them.

MIKE: What if the guy I say it to says that he doesn't care if I get hurt?

TEACHER: Good question. There are some people out there who have a hard time hearing that they have hurt other people, so they try to defend themselves by saying they don't care. Well, then you could say, "I had you figured wrong; I thought you were the kind of guy who cared about other people's feelings."

MIKE: Okay.

TEACHER: What do you say again, if he says that he doesn't care if he hurt your feelings?

MIKE: Something like, "Oh, I was thinking that you would care about other people."

TEACHER: Good job!

MIKE: What if I forget the first part of what I'm supposed to say?

TEACHER: No problem! These "I" messages take a little practice. Just stop by and we'll practice it again.

MIKE: Okay, but I think I'm going to try it today, before I forget.

TEACHER: Wow, you really are a smart and strong kid. Good luck!

MIKE: Thanks!

Negative Assertion

nother great way to respond to putdowns is to agree. This is called "negative assertion," because we assert, or bring attention to, the negative. This technique is effective, because it takes a healthy person to admit that he has weaknesses or lapses. This raises the score of the person being put down, thus *increasing* the discrepancy between the scores. This is not what the person saying the putdown is hoping for. Remember, he's hoping for the opposite. He's hoping that the person being put down will act in a foolish, childish or immature way, thus *decreasing* the discrepancy between the two perceived scores.

WHAT ARE SOME EXAMPLES OF NEGATIVE ASSERTION?

EXAMPLES OF THIS TECHNIQUE ABOUND. IT IS RELATIVELY EASY TO DO AND OFTEN BEGINS WITH WORDS LIKE:

- "Good point!"
- "True."
- "Probably so!"
- "You're right!"
- "I agree!"
- "I know."

And can be extended to:

- "You can say that again!"
- "Who could argue with that?"
- "You took the words right out of my mouth!"
- "Just what I was thinking!"
- "That's not the first time I've heard that today!"

- "I know, I often am ... "
- "That, too!" As in:

"You look ugly today" ... "Isn't it amazing that I even left the house looking like this?"

"And you look fat!" ... *"I know; that, too!"*

Many times, agreeing is all that is necessary! However, the person responding to the putdown may choose to elaborate. Perhaps the best example of this is from the classic book, *Cyrano de Bergerac*, which was made into the film *Roxeanne*. The main character has an inordinately huge nose. A man in a bar comments on it by saying, "What a big nose you have!" The hero responds, "What a missed opportunity! With a nose like this, is that all you can say?" Then he proceeds to give twenty examples of putdowns that would have been more clever, such as, "Tell me, with a nose like that, can you smell the coffee ... in Brazil?" By the time he's finished, the person who originally criticized him is humiliated, and the others listening are applauding the hero. Why is this so effective? Because the hero has the ability to agree that his nose is big, to laugh at his inadequacies. This shows a strong and healthy person, far healthier than the person who started all the nonsense. Eventually, the perpetrator has to leave, because his goal of feeling better about himself has not been met; in fact, he clearly feels worse!

I had a blind date once with a man who said, "You got that right!" after just about everything I said. "Beautiful day today, wasn't it?" "You got that right!" "Boy, Denver has sure grown in the last few years, hasn't it?" "You got that right!" "This soup is delicious!" "You got that right!" It didn't make for an enticing conversation, but it struck me that "You got that right" could be used as a wonderful negative assertion!

I hear professional athletes do this all the time, and it strikes me that they have developed, probably because of years of teamwork, a real ability "to roll with the punches." I heard a radio announcer ask Reggie Rivers, a former Bronco, "And when you go there tonight, why don't you do something about your wardrobe?" Reggie answered, "Great idea! I'll see what I can do."

The next night, I heard Scott Hastings talking with Floyd Little, a great former Bronco running back. Scott kidded with him by saying, "The only reason you got so many yards rushing is because you were so bowlegged!" Floyd rolled with the punch and answered in a heartbeat, chuckling, "That's right! No tackler could get both arms around my bow-legs!"

There was an exchange on the KOA Sports Zoo radio show that exemplified this principle. One commentator said, "You look tired." The other answered kiddingly, "Yeah, but I can get rest, while you'll still be ugly." The first answered with a negative assertion, "You ain't kiddin!"

Another powerful example happened at my school. Three coaches were walking down the hall. One of them asserted, "Dan, George could kick your butt!" Dan snapped back, "Oh, I already know that!" By the way, Dan is a mass of muscle, similar to what you would see on the cover of *Muscle Magazine.* George, too, is very athletic and strong. What's key here is Dan had nothing to prove, so it was easy for him to roll with the taunt. It was a lighthearted tease, not intended to hurt anyone's feelings, but I was impressed with how quickly Dan exemplified the effective response of a healthy adult with a strong self-concept.

We have a lot to gain from these athletes who have learned so successfully how to work on a team and how to respond to this kind of comment. It's true that many times the comment is just meant to be kidding, but a person who is less healthy could take it personally and respond defensively. That surely would aggravate the situation.

A favorite thing for students to say in class is, "This is boring!" Jim Fay taught me a great response to this, "I know, isn't it? But you ought to see me in the afternoon; I'm really putting kids to sleep by then!" Of course, I could also say, "You've got that right!"

"Looks like you've gained five pounds!" "No, actually, I think it's ten!" This starts with a disagreement, but then the negative was asserted to a greater degree than it was proposed in the first place: ten pounds instead of five!

One time I had a student who had really thin legs. On a warm spring day, he wore shorts to school. Another student went up to him and said, "You have really skinny legs!" He responded, "I know it! Look, my bicep is almost bigger than my thigh!" The other student said, "Yeah," then walked away.

My mother taught English as a second language at Denver University. She tells the story of a teacher who said, "Mohammed always sleeps in my class!" Another teacher responded with the somewhat nasty comment, "That's funny, he never sleeps in mine!" The first, obviously healthy teacher replied, "That must be because he gets so much rest in my class!"

Sometimes when we play a game in class, students will say to me (the referee), "You like them better. You're favoring their answers!" I answer, "True. I especially like them better now!"

This is a great technique for parents. If your son says, "Mom, you like Mindy better!" Agree and say, "Sometimes true, but especially now!" (It's only human and honest to admit that *at times* a parent would like one child better than the other.)

Or, it works well for kids when their parents are being critical. One of my students said that his mom accused him of being selfish. He answered, "I know, I've been working on it." She added, "And you've been lazy lately!" He quipped, "I know; that, too!" That was enough for her, she had no come-back.

I heard a great example of a negative assertion while I was flying on a Mexicana flight to Puerto Vallarta. A woman said to the flight attendant in Spanish, "You men are all alike!" He answered, "Yes! Except some of us are worse!" They both laughed.

Once I was teaching this concept of agreeing with the putdown to sixth graders. One student told another, "Your mother wears combat boots." The task of the put-down student was to respond with a negative assertion. He answered, "Yes, and did you realize that she sleeps in them?"

I've seen people trip or "mess up" and just say, "How am I doing?" And laugh it off.

The idea of a negative assertion is not being afraid to pay attention to a weakness or mistake.

Here's another great teacher one: A kid asks in algebra class, "When am I ever going to use this?" Teacher answers, "You're not!" (The teacher is agreeing that the information is useless. End of discussion. It's impossible to argue with that, even though we know it isn't true.)

I heard a teacher tell another teacher one morning: "Hey, you're getting a pretty healthy bald spot there, Bill!" Bill answered, "Yep, it's so shiny my wife uses my head as a mirror to put on her lipstick in the morning!"

Another colleague once said to a secretary, "Gee, you don't look too good today, Doris." She quipped, "You should have seen me yesterday!"

"Is that your second cookie?" "No, I think it's my fourth or fifth!" (Again, I'm asserting something even more negative than you're proposing: four or five cookies instead of just two.)

I was kidding with a student assistant of mine one time and asked him, "What's wrong with you?" He came back with, "Oh, lots of stuff!" This struck me as a wonderful negative assertion that could be used with a true putdown.

When I taught middle school, I had a student named Paul who was really well-liked by other kids. One day, another student came up to him and said in a somewhat nasty, you're-not-so-cool tone, "I have that same exact shirt!" Paul asserted the negative by responding, "Yes, but did your mother get it in the wrong load of wash so that it has bleach stains on it like mine does?" Student number one was left somewhat speechless, but not disgraced or embarrassed. No wonder other kids liked Paul so well. He was able to laugh at himself, didn't find it necessary to try to impress others, and could roll with the punches. He clearly won this round, while not antagonizing the other kid.

Several years ago, a student named Susie came to me very upset.

She reported that her best friend, Michelle, wanted to beat her up (... something about Michelle's boyfriend liking Susie now instead of Michelle ...) Michelle wanted to get in a fight with Susie and settle the situation once and for all. But Susie didn't want to fight her; in fact she wanted to stay friends with her! I asked her what she had tried, and she mentioned all the usual stuff. She had tried ignoring it, she had cried and said she didn't want to fight, and she had tried to avoid her—all to no avail. Michelle stayed after her. I remembered something that Jim Fay had taught me a few years before. I said, "Well, are you ready to try something crazy?" She said, "Sure!"

I suggested, "Agree with her! Say that you would really rather be her friend, but if Michelle felt that she must fight, how hard did she intend to hit? Should Susie wear protective clothing and have an ambulance waiting in the wings? Would it be on school grounds where they were likely to be suspended, or could they do it off school boundaries?"

Susie agreed that it sounded like a fun thing to try. She did. It worked! Michelle said, "What, are you crazy?" and walked away. Several days later, they re-established their friendship. Can you believe it? But I can't tell you what happened with the boyfriend ...

I had an Italian student who was a member of the football team. The day before a game, the team often wore shirts and ties and nice slacks. My Italian student chose to wear black pants, a black shirt, and a white tie. A classmate turned to him and said, "You look like a gangster!" The astute football player answered, "I'm in the mafia; don't mess with me!" The other student smiled and left him alone.

Here's another great example of a negative assertion: High school students love to spread sexual rumors about their peers, especially about the cute girls who are well-liked by the boys. Sandy, one of my student assistants, experienced this one Monday morning. A kid came up to her and said, "I heard what you did this weekend!" Sandy didn't miss a beat as she answered, "Yes, but did you hear about how we got in the hot tub and joined the other couple with the whipped cream?" This was too much for the student trying to get her goat, and she walked away saying, "Humph!" No one spread rumors about Sandy again. They just didn't work.

I remembered this story when another female student came to me saying that some kids were spreading terrible rumors about what she was doing with her boyfriend, and the stories weren't true. She told me that she had tried denying them; in fact, she had started a campaign to prove these rumors were false, but it just made things worse. (Sure, it would. Remember, defending and proving normally just escalate the situation.)

I said, "Ready to try something wild?" She said, "Sure!" I recommended that she try agreeing with them. Ironically, a boy came up to my desk when I was talking to Sandy and said, "I heard about you and your boyfriend and the sleazy stuff you've been doing." She didn't miss a beat and retorted, "Yep! Wanna be next?" The boy bolted in surprise, then walked quickly away with a baffled look on his face. She was delighted that her response had worked; she winked and smiled at me. I got a tremendous kick out of her answer, but I have a word of caution. Her answer was very effective in this case, but it is not one I would always recommend, because with high school boys, you never know ...

It can be very important to use the word "sometimes" in negative assertion. If someone says you're stupid, you don't want to agree and say, "I know I am." But you can say, "So true! *Sometimes* I can do really stupid stuff!" There's a powerful implied message here, *"Sometimes* I do really smart stuff!" And that is what being human is all about.

Often, you don't feel like agreeing with the putdown. Let's say someone says they think your dress is ugly, but you like your dress. I wouldn't recommend you agree in this situation. This is a great time for a neutral response, "Oh, thanks for your input." Or, "Oh, that hurts; I've always liked this dress." Or suppose a student accuses you of being a terrible teacher. I would not suggest that you diminish yourself in such an important area by agreeing. You can use one of the other techniques you'll read about in upcoming chapters.

Frequently, people throw putdowns out in the form of a question, like, "Where did you get that dress?" Or, "Why did you wear that dress today?" These are tricky, because we don't really know, until we clarify, what the person actually means. She could be interested in buying one like it, and would like to hear the name of the store.

Or, she might be hinting that you shouldn't shop at thrift stores. Here's what to do. Try to open up the hidden message by asking "Oh, don't you like my dress?" If the answer is, "Yes, I love it, I just wanted to know where I could get one like it," you're home free. If it's, "Nope, I think it's really unattractive on you," then you can slide into any great response to putdowns.

WAYS TO MESS UP NEGATIVE ASSERTIONS

As with any technique, sarcasm, anger, a nasty tone of voice or negative, controlling body language will make negative assertions ineffective, as will insincerity in admitting that you have a weakness. The ability to laugh at oneself is a definite asset to delivering negative assertions effectively. Have fun with this technique. Enjoy yourself!

A person who can celebrate his accomplishments and strengths as well as laugh at his occasional miscues and mistakes is likely to be a very joyful and healthy individual.

WHEN ARE THE BEST TIMES TO USE NEGATIVE ASSERTIONS?

Negative assertion is a great technique for the times you've been hit with a "medium" or "light" putdown; that is, one that doesn't cut you to the quick, and one where the issue is not of great importance. So, if you say my hair looks bad today, that's not a very big deal, and it's easy to agree that some days it looks like I combed it with a pinecone. Of course, if we all were totally unafraid of being inadequate, it would be easy to roll with all putdowns or criticism.

There is another form of negative assertion that can be used to signal a very healthy person. Suppose you're walking with your boyfriend at the mall and he spots a foxy girl walking by. He says, "Whew! What a fox!" You respond with, "Boy, she is pretty, isn't she!" This statement packs a wallop. It says:

I'm so healthy that I don't have to compete with other women. I am so confident that I am attractive, I can acknowledge that other women are pretty, too. I do not need constant flattery and applause from you in order to feel good about myself. I can handle it when you compliment others. I'm not about to get into a control battle with you, saying things like, "You shouldn't be looking at other women; you should only have eyes for me!" This could be exactly what he is looking for ... to push your button and fire up a defensive response from you. This could be an invitation to a big fight.

People Magazine published an article about Jackie Kennedy Onassis that illustrated this form of negative assertion. The story tells of a time in 1973 when Jackie was experiencing many difficulties. Whereas she was noted for her extraordinary good looks and style, one day she was particularly sad and distraught. She appeared at a luncheon engagement in an unflattering dress, no make-up and a scarf covering her undone hair. Ari Onassis attacked her and said, "Look at you; how can you be seen like that? You don't see Gloria and Aileen in that kind of get-up. What is your problem?" Jackie didn't miss a beat. She smiled her brightest smile and answered, "Yes, don't they look great!" This is a form of negative assertion. She was, in fact, agreeing with part of her husband's putdown and compliment of the other women. She handled this awkward incident with grace, preserving her dignity while making her husband look bad for the insensitive comment.

TEACHER: Jennifer, I'm glad you came by.

JENNIFER: You said you'd help me come up with some things to say when kids make fun of my nose.

TEACHER: Happy to! In fact, we're in luck. I grew up in a family where we were all given pretty healthy sized noses. So I had lots of practice as a kid, and I got to hear my brother handle teasing about his nose, also.

JENNIFER So what did you all do?

TEACHER: We just agreed with people. Sometimes we even added on to what they said. Like, if someone said, "Wow, that's quite a schnoz you've got," my brother would say, "I know, isn't it? One time I got a bee sting on the end of it, and it was about the size of Montana. You should have seen it then!"

JENNIFER It's kind of hard for me to laugh about it ... but I think I could try it.

TEACHER: My guess is that if you try it, you'll find it gets easier every time. And pretty soon, people will forget to bug you about it!

JENNIFER Why does this work?

TEACHER: Because it takes such a healthy person to laugh at himself, and the teaser is hoping for an immature or unhealthy response, like retaliating, crying, fighting, etc. If the guy who started it can make the other guy look or, better yet, *act* like an idiot, he feels powerful and in control. But if you can respond in a light and healthy way, it makes *him* look bad! He'll have to go look for another target, one who will respond the way he wants.

JENNIFER So what if I can't think of anything right away?

TEACHER: You don't have to be fancy or really witty. Just agree with what he says. Like, "I know, isn't it?" Or, "That's not the first time I've heard that today! Or, "So true!" Make sure you don't sound sarcastic though! If you can muster up a chuckle, that's even better.

JENNIFER Could I say, "You ought to see my dad's nose? It's even bigger than mine?"

TEACHER: Sure. That's exactly the idea! You know, now that you're all armed and ready with a healthy response, don't be surprised if you *don't* get a chance to use it.

JENNIFER Why is that?

TEACHER: I'm not sure, but I've seen it happen a million times. Seems like when a kid gets all ready to roll with the punches, they don't get thrown. Maybe it's a strength that other people pick up intuitively. Either way, you'll be ready. And you might find it kind of fun! Let me know what happens, okay?

JENNIFER Okay.

TEACHER: And good luck!

JENNIFER Thanks.

Neutral Responses

nother great way to respond to putdowns or power struggles is the strategy of using a *neutral response.* A neutral response says, "I heard you, I value your opinion, but I don't choose to give my own opinion of your comment," and "I don't choose to engage in a power struggle with you!" You are neither agreeing nor disagreeing with the person's observation.

Like "I" messages, neutral responses are best done with a non-sarcastic, soft voice, and relaxed, non-controlling or aggressive body language. *This is very important!* Otherwise, they can sound like snappy, sarcastic or snobby retorts!

Neutral responses are effective, because you are not allowing the other person to "get" to you, causing you to respond in an inappropriate or immature way. If he is trying to push your button, you are not allowing it to ring your bell! In addition, you are saying that you are open to suggestion and criticism. This takes a very healthy and mature person. Again, you are causing your score to climb, rather than descend. If you were to respond in an immature or unhealthy way, you would lower your score, exactly what the aggressor may be looking for. In addition, this particular technique sends the implied message that the person making the inappropriate comment is actually trying to be helpful. (In some situations, this may actually be true.)

I first discovered the effectiveness of neutral responses when I was out jogging one day. I have never been a great runner, and my pace would not threaten Frank Shorter. In fact, I have always felt a little self-conscious about jogging. One day, I was out trotting in an unfamiliar neighborhood. A man in a truck drove by. He was smoking a cigarette and drinking a beer and yelled out the window to me, "Run faster! You need to!" Ouch! That really hit my button, because I was especially sensitive in this arena. I wanted to respond with that familiar, internationally understood obscene gesture, but I caught myself. I did *not* want to lower myself to his level or allow him to ring my bell. So I gathered together my senses and my friendliest tone of voice and answered with, "Thanks for telling me! I'll remember that!"

The look on his face was unforgettable. Bewildered. Baffled. "She'll remember that?" I just know that my response was not what he expected, and I could imagine him driving away thinking about that crazy woman who was going to "remember that." See, that's what you want to do, leave 'em thinking!

In addition, I felt proud of myself that I didn't lower myself to his level. It would have been easy to point out that he was drinking and smoking and would probably die prematurely if he didn't begin an exercise program himself. But that would have been a cruel and hurtful thing to say and certainly wouldn't have made me feel better about myself. I believe that it is impossible to feel great about yourself while being cruel to, or inconsiderate of, others.

Sharon Salzberg, a foremost American religious teacher was quoted as saying in the April 1998 issue of *American Health,*

> **"The basis of self-respect is morality. We're so connected with one another that if we hurt somebody, that hurts us, too."**

Another reason neutral responses are effective is that they are easy to learn and use. I recommend that people get a favorite response, memorize and practice it, then have it ready. So many people say that they can't think of a great retort at the time of the offense, but they do think of something clever and wonderful hours later. (However, I've noticed that most often what they think of later is usually something caustic or sarcastic, such as, "Well, if you had friends, you would spend time on the phone, too!") Whenever you feel that you have been criticized or put down but can't think of something magnificent to reply, it's a perfect time for a "neutral response." It may not be the very best thing you could say, but at least it will keep you from engaging and lowering your score, and it will almost definitely leave the other person thinking. They'll probably be thinking something like, "What?" or "Wow, that didn't work quite like I planned ..."

WHAT ARE SOME EXAMPLES OF NEUTRAL RESPONSES?

Neutral responses say, "I heard you. I'll consider your input. I'm healthy enough to change and grow, and I may use your comment for that purpose. Or, I may not! But, I value *you*, and your opinion. I may or may not agree. And I do not intend to argue!"

EXAMPLES:

- "Thanks for telling me!"
- "I'll remember that!"
- "I'm sorry you see it that way."
- "That's good information for me."
- "That's a point."
- "That's a thought." (Everything is a thought; we're just not commenting on the value of this one ...)
- "It's good to know your perspective."
- "Thanks for your opinion."
- "Good to know how you see it."
- "I appreciate your letting me know."
- "I value the information!"
- "Interesting perspective!"

As you can see, sarcasm would totally defeat the healthy purpose of these responses.

It's important to be honest and sincere, because that's what conveys the information that you are healthy enough to accept suggestion or criticism. You genuinely mean that you value the information.

I have found there are times when someone says something to me that I could interpret as a putdown, which in fact is helpful information to me. For example, I appreciate it when my students tell me that my slip is showing or that I have lipstick on my teeth. It truly is good information for me to have, so I can correct the situation. I wouldn't want to go through a day with bad breath or toilet paper sticking to my shoe! If I demonstrate that I am healthy enough to accept constructive criticism, then I can feel confident that my friends won't allow me to progress through life with a piece of spinach stuck between my teeth!

You may be wondering, "Yeah, but what about when someone who isn't a friend tells you something like this?" Anyone who can respond in this way is likely to develop a friend! For example, you say, "Wow, thanks for telling me!" It's pretty hard for the other person to not feel accepted by you. Even if you say, "I'm sorry you feel that way," you are validating the other guys' feelings, which is another way of sending the implied message, *"I accept you and your opinions, even though I may not agree."*

When people know that I will welcome their input, they won't feel threatened to tell me next time. Beneath this, there is a deep understanding that we are all part of the human condition. We all make mistakes. We all have embarrassing things happen to us. We all have weaknesses. There are things about us that other people don't accept. And it's all okay! We can laugh at ourselves and welcome opportunities for growth. Not everyone needs to like everything about us. It is in this spirit that the neutral response should be delivered.

Neutral responses are particularly useful when you just don't know what to say. Later, when you get home, you think of a million things you could have answered. Memorize a neutral response that feels good to you, and have it handy for those occasions when you're at a loss for words.

WAYS TO MESS UP NEUTRAL RESPONSES

Use a sarcastic tone of voice, angry or aggressive body language, cry or whine. Otherwise, they are pretty foolproof.

WHEN IS THE BEST TIME TO USE THEM?

The best time to use neutral responses is when you don't agree with the comment, but it isn't a big enough issue to use an "I" message or to say, "Tell me more." Again, they are also great to use in the "hit and run" situation ... when you need something to say quickly!

DAD: So, Jimmy, how's it going with translating what kids are saying to you?

JIMMY: Pretty good. Most of the time I remember to do it. It helps me to think about it differently, but I'd really like them to stop saying mean stuff.

DAD: I don't blame you. Well, one thing you can do is agree with what they are saying.

JIMMY: I don't want to agree with things that aren't true.

DAD: Great point; me, neither. So, I have another idea.

JIMMY: Good, because I need a good one.

DAD: You can use what we call a "neutral response."

JIMMY: What's that?

DAD: Well, it's where you stay calm and don't get sarcastic. Do you know what that means?

JIMMY: Not exactly …

DAD: Sarcasm is when you get a nasty tone in your voice and kind of make fun of them back. You might say good words, but the way you say them sounds like you don't really mean what you're saying.

JIMMY: I think I know what you mean.

DAD: So you get a nice, soft, happy tone of voice, and you say something like, "Thanks for telling me!" or, "It's good to know how you see it." or, "I'll remember that!" Want to practice it?

JIMMY: Sure.

DAD: Say something nasty to me, and I'll show you how to do it.

JIMMY: Okay, "Dad, you're really a creep!"

DAD: "Thanks for telling me. It's good to know how you see it."

JIMMY: This is sort of fun.

DAD: Try another one!

JIMMY: Okay, "You're fat and gross!"

DAD: "I'm sorry you feel that way."

JIMMY: Wow. When you answer like that, it doesn't leave me much to say.

DAD: Exactly! Now let's try it the other way. I'll put you down, and you give me a nice, kind, neutral answer. You want to show me that you've heard me, you're not mad, but you don't necessarily agree.

JIMMY: Ready!

DAD: "Boy, that is an ugly shirt you have on!"

JIMMY: You bought it for me! Oops! I forgot. I mean, "Good to know that you don't like my shirt."

DAD: There you go! Want to try another one?

JIMMY: Nope, I think I've got it. Whatever they say, I just say something like, "Thanks for letting me know." Or, "That's good information."

DAD: Exactly. Now get out there and try this the next time you are put down.

JIMMY: You're so goofy, Dad.

DAD: Thanks for telling me!

Outcrazy the Crazies

What does it mean to outcrazy the crazies, and why is it effective? Outcrazying the crazies is perhaps the most fun and most bizarre of all the techniques. Foster Cline, a nationally acclaimed psychiatrist and consultant, always asserted that there is not room in the same place for two crazy people. So if a crazy person comes up to you—one who is being unkind, wildly irrational, or using a putdown—you can raise the odds tremendously that he will soon leave if you simply act crazier than him. The other reason that this works is that you are stating in no uncertain terms that you just are not going to engage in this lowly discussion. So you just do something crazy in response to the putdown or power struggle.

EXAMPLES:

PUTDOWN: "You're ugly."

OUTCRAZY: (bark like a dog!)

PUTDOWN: "It's stupid that the school store is out of my favorite candy!"

OUTCRAZY: "The gypsies stole my dog!"

I worked with a man, Rocco Rofrano, who was a master at this. He taught seventh-grade social studies. One day I was walking by his classroom and I saw one of his students go up to his desk and say, "This test is unfair! It's too hard!" Rocco answered, "Go lie down now, go lie down." And the little seventh grader went away. Sometimes he would say, in the same situation, "I'll bring the tortilla chips!"

My favorite, and the name of the video I made on this topic, is called, "No thanks, I just had a banana."

Elementary students intuitively know about this when they repeat what the other kid has said. The conversation often goes something like this:

CHILD #1: "You're ugly"

CHILD # 2: "You're ugly!"

CHILD # 1: "Quit repeating me!"

CHILD #2: "Quit repeating me!"

CHILD # 1: "You're driving me crazy!"

CHILD #2: "You're driving me crazy!"

Usually, at this point, Child #1 says "Arghh!" and goes away, while Child #2 smiles to himself and repeats one last time, "Arghh!"

I was teaching how to outcrazy the crazies to a group of teachers. When it was time to practice, the plan was for everyone to write a putdown on a card. Then they would get in pairs, pass the cards around, say the putdowns, and answer with an "outcrazy." One member of the class was a shy, lady-like elementary school teacher. The first card handed to her said, "You're ugly." She was all prepared with an outcrazy. She retorted, "No thanks, I just had a banana." The next card she was handed said, "You're selfish." She answered, "No thanks, I just had a banana." The next card said, "Asshole!" She stuck with her standard outcrazy and said, "No thanks, I just had a banana!"

There is a great Gary Larson *Far Side* cartoon that shows a bizarre, eight-legged, four-clawed space-like creature climbing in the window of a house. The family dog is standing by and upon seeing this creature, states, "Whoa! Maybe I'll just pass on my usual barking frenzy!" Clearly the dog understands that there is no way he can outcrazy *this* creature!

My father once got a random obscene phone call at three in the morning. The callers ranted and raved. My father said in a very calm tone, "Well, I'm going to have to let you fellas go now. Bye." Last phone call he got from them!

The sky is the limit on outcrazy comments. Animal imitations and beeping computer sounds are good. Singing is effective. I like also to use trite expressions like, "Hey there, that's my baby!" or, "I've been down that road before."

I had a student who was a master of this technique. Alissa would say, "One, two, three, giraffe," while counting with her fingers. No one could ever figure out what she was doing exactly, but it sure worked!

OTHER WINNERS:
- "I don't know what got in to me."
- "We're gonna take 'em one game at a time."
- "Tomorrow is another day."
- "Well, life is short, you know." (If you'd really like to baffle 'em you could add, "but wide!")
- "Where does the time go?"
- "I love Paris in the springtime ..."
- "Think it's gonna rain?"
- "Doesn't that just frost 'ya?" (This one can be really fun to say ... and there's something undefinably wonderful about it, too.)
- "Well, I'm just not as young as I used to be" (This is multi-purpose and somehow extra powerful! It's kind of an outcrazy combined with a negative assertion; that is, "You look terrible today! "Well, I'm just not as young as I used to be." Of course, this is true for anyone, because even ten-year-olds are always older today than they were the day before.)

- "I hate it when that happens!" As in: "You look fat!" "I hate it when that happens!"
- Or, use the Steven Wright thought: "It's a small world, but I wouldn't want to paint it ..."
- Or begin a joke: "So a guy walks into a bar ..."
- Respond in a foreign language or Pig Latin.

Mais ce qui me frappe c'est que le temps fait si beau aujourd'hui!

¡Saludos, amigos!

I have an adult friend who says, "Oh, huh!" (That's a pretty crazy thing for an adult to say, as in, "This class is boring!" "Oh, huh!"

In the movie, *Breakfast Club*, Bender (the tough guy) is making fun of the unpopular student named Brian. He says, "Who's your dad? Mr. Rogers?" Brian aptly responds in a calm voice: "No. Mr. Johnson." That's kind of crazy! And it leaves Bender without a reply.

I have a student named Chris who told me that one day a husky boy had come up to him saying that he was going to beat him up. Chris responded by laughing hysterically. (That's a pretty crazy thing to do after a threat like that, no?) He acted like it was just a big joke, patted the guy on the back and walked off. It worked. The fight never happened.

Sharon, a dear friend of mine, has a mother who has been difficult to deal with for over fifty years. Sharon had tried everything and finally realized that being reasonable simply didn't work. After fifty years of trying to be rational with her, Sharon finally happened on a miraculous way to handle her mother. She started to outcrazy her.

Sharon's mom was complaining that her son (Sharon's brother) was trying to cheat her out of her money while doing her taxes. In the past Sharon would have argued and reminded her mom how loving and helpful her brother had been. This time, Sharon answered, "You're right! He's a scoundrel! What other explanation can there be? I can't believe how unscrupulous he's being! I'm going to call him right now and straighten him out!"

Her mom was shocked and answered, "Oh, now, no need to be so hasty, I bet it was just an oversight on his part," and she backed off.

The next day, Sharon went to visit her mom in her retirement home. Her mom started in again about how Sharon never came to visit her, saying, "I'll bet you'll never spend more time with me. I will probably be dead before you ever quit your job and visit more often!" Sharon didn't miss a beat and quipped, "You've got it! You finally understand, Mom!" A dazed mom had nothing left to say.

Another time, Sharon had taken her overly picky mother shopping. After hours of sorting through clothes, her mom finally found a pant suit she liked, but it needed to be altered. The department store said it would be happy to do the alterations, but there would be a charge. Her mom stormed out of the store, insisting that it was ridiculous that the alterations weren't free. Sharon, frazzled by this point, began to argue, stating that stores no longer did alterations for free, asking her mom why she didn't want to keep the lovely outfit and pay for the alterations. After making the discovery of how effective it was to outcrazy her mom, Sharon took her mom shopping once again. The entire scene was reenacted. But this time, Sharon said, "You're right! We're not ever coming back here, and especially not to buy that outfit you love. We're not giving them our business! They're cheap and selfish in this store!" Her mom, accustomed to seizing the opposite position, demanded that they buy the outfit and pay for it to be altered. Sharon has found that interacting with her mom has become much more enjoyable!

A variation of this is the famous Jim Fay line. When a child says he is going to run away, you just answer, "I'll love you, Honey, no matter where you live!"

I grew up in a neighborhood with a very clever woman. One day, a little girl came running up to her to tattle on the woman's daughter. She said, "Your daughter just did this bad thing and said this mean thing to so and so, and then she did this evil thing." The clever mom snapped, "Well, that does it! Now I'm definitely not having that party my daughter was going to invite *you* to!"

I had a conversation the other day with a witty teacher named Penny. She was talking with a student who was complaining that he didn't have enough time to do his homework. "But I work from 3:00 P.M. until 8:30 P.M.! When am I supposed to do all this homework?" he grumbled. The common comeback from most teachers would have been, "Well, it looks like you need to quit your job or cut down your hours! You need to get your priorities straight!" Penny, however, didn't miss the opportunity to outcrazy. She said, "I have an idea! Maybe you should quit school. That will give you more time to work and get ahead in your job."

This technique must be used without sarcasm, or it will sound really nasty. Why was her response effective here? Because we all know, especially the kid, that it is crazy to ask a teacher not to assign math homework because the student works after school. He realizes (I promise that he does) that this is his choice and he must manage his time to fit in homework!

WAYS TO MESS UP AN OUTCRAZY

Act hesitant or meek. You need to assert your craziness and leave no doubt. Probably the only thing to remember here is that you don't want to use outcrazies all the time. Why? People will think you're crazy!

WHEN ARE THE BEST TIMES TO USE OUTCRAZIES?

Probably it's best not to use this technique with someone you're trying to impress, or someone who has power over you. It's a great technique for people who are being wildly irrational, for people who aren't listening, or for those who are droning on and on. The crazier the other person is acting, the more you know it's a great time to *outcrazy them!*

SUSIE: Mom, today I talked with my teacher about how Kristen has been acting. She really helped me understand what is going on. She said that even though Kristen looks like she's doing fine, she is probably having a tough time with her parents' separation. I understand that, and I feel really badly for her, but now she has a new friend who is really strange! She does and says the weirdest things to me!

MOM: So, she does pretty crazy stuff?

SUSIE: Yep! Like today she repeated everything I said. I haven't heard that since elementary school. Then she started making fun of my clothes. And she just wouldn't stop. It was SO weird! And it hurt my feelings. I just didn't know what to do about her.

MOM: Sounds like time for one of my favorite techniques, "outcrazy the crazies."

SUSIE: What's that?

MOM: Well, if you're ready to have some fun and you're not afraid to look a little goofy, here's the plan. You just do something crazier than she's doing! Like when she starts criticizing your clothes, just start singing your favorite song. Or make animal noises. Or repeat the slogan of a favorite commercial. My favorite has always been, "No thanks, I just had a banana!"

SUSIE: You mean I just say that?

MOM: Yep!

SUSIE: Why does this work?

MOM: There's an unspoken psychological rule that there isn't room for two crazy people in the same place. If you act crazier that the other guy, the other guy has to go away!

SUSIE: Weird!

MOM: It also works because it says that you aren't willing to "get into it" with the other guy. It says that you just won't respond negatively to their weird or nasty behavior.

SUSIE: Sounds kind of fun.

MOM: Yes, it's a fun thing to do now and then. But you don't want to do it all the time. Know why?

SUSIE: Because then everyone would really start to think I was crazy?

MOM: Exactly!

SUSIE: Well, I have nothing to lose!

MOM: I agree. Good luck!

Broken Record and Tell Me More

nother effective way to respond to putdowns is the "broken record" technique. I learned this from Jim Fay, who is an absolute master at this skill. Pick a positive, non-defensive, friendly, adult-sounding message, and repeat it using a soft tone and normal-colored face. It's effective, because it keeps you from engaging with the content of the other person's message, and you are not displaying any anger or negative reaction to their tacky comment. It's likely to leave the other guy thinking, too! "Broken record" clearly says, "I'm not about to lose my cool or get into an argument or power struggle with you." You might also be able to include a positive thought which can have a powerful effect on the sender.

EXAMPLES:

Use any effective response (including the one presented previously) and repeat it, each time allowing your voice to get softer and softer.

- "You're ugly." *"It's good to know how you see it!"*
- "And I hate you!" *"It's good to know how you see it."*
- "You're fat, too!" *"It's good to know how you see it."*
- Or, "I hate this class!" *"Sorry you feel that way."*
- And I hate you, too!" *"Sorry you feel that way."*

Or, start with a neutral statement, then add a positive message and repeat it, each time allowing your voice to get softer.

"I hate you!" Broken record: *"That may be, but I'd like to be your friend!"*

The "I'd like to be your friend" part is a new addition. That's the positive message that will probably be very powerful. Why? Few people can look someone else in the eye and answer, "No way, I won't be your friend!" That  message will probably *not* be effective if it is delivered to a group of people. They might very well answer, "Great! But, we don't want to be *your* friend." This response is much tougher for an individual to say when he's alone with you. Should he respond negatively, however, it's time to reply, "Well, no problem, I just wanted you to know that I'd like to be your friend," and walk away. Rare would be the person who wouldn't feel some serious guilt at this point!

"But you're weird!" *"That may be, but I'd like to be your friend."*

"But you're driving me crazy!" *"That may be, but I'd like to be your friend."*

"I'm outta here!" *"That may be, but I'd like to be your friend."*

Teachers can use this when a child needs to be temporarily removed from the classroom. They can say to the student,

"You're welcome back as soon as your behavior is appropriate."

"But I didn't do anything!" *"Yes, and you're welcome back as soon as your behavior is appropriate!"*

"But she started it!" (Softer voice:) *"Could be, and you're welcome back as soon as your behavior is appropriate."*

"This is unfair!" (Still softer voice:) *"Could be, and you're welcome back as soon as your behavior is appropriate."*

"Sometimes I can't stand this class!" (Softer yet ...) *"Can't wait to have you back as soon as your behavior is appropriate."*

It's not necessary that the message be an exact repeat every time. Notice the positive messages here: "Welcome back" means "I like you! and I welcome *you* to be in class, it's just that behavior I won't tolerate." "Can't wait to have you back" is an even more powerful expression of affection for the student.

I have discovered that even if the student attempts to keep arguing, eventually the rest of the class will say, "Will you get outta here?" All the while, the teacher remains calm with a slight smile on his face, and then proceeds with teaching.

Remember Sharon, the one with the difficult mother? Her mom has always been controlling, and she insists on her way without consideration of Sharon's needs. Her mom had been nagging Sharon to take her to Kansas. Sharon, who is an active working woman, finally made plans to take her mother to Kansas. She called (prepared for a battle) and informed her, "I can go to Kansas with you Tuesday." Her mom snapped, "Well, it's never a good idea to buy tickets less than three weeks in advance!" Sharon answered, "I can go to Kansas with you Tuesday." Her mom came back with, "I thought we'd go the end of June!" "I can go to Kansas with you Tuesday." "We won't be able to get a rental car with such short notice!" "I can go to Kansas with you on Tuesday." "I have things planned, I'd have to change them!" "I can go to Kansas with you on Tuesday." Her mom's protests continued for a while, but Sharon stuck to her guns.

They went on Tuesday.

WAYS TO MESS UP THE BROKEN RECORD

A way to mess up the "broken record" is to have sarcasm in your voice, change the message a great deal, or get angry and louder as you repeat the message.

WHEN ARE THE BEST TIMES TO USE THE BROKEN RECORD?

This technique can help to avoid potential power struggles, or it can be used in situations where you think the person might stay after you and argue or defend his position. It's very effective with demanding or argumentative folks, or when you suspect that a battle could ensue.

"TELL ME MORE"—WHAT IS IT, AND WHY IS IT EFFECTIVE?

Someone issues a putdown or criticism. You respond by saying something such as "Tell me more," which invites the other person to point out more weaknesses or areas that need improvement.

By now, it should be apparent why these are such powerful tools. Anyone who is so healthy that he can actually invite *more* criticism is certainly not someone who is a good target for a putdown! This response shows that the person who was criticized is *way* too healthy for the average cheap shot artist. In addition, it can be a great way to problem-solve and grow, without becoming defensive.

HERE ARE SOME EXAMPLES.

Let's say that your husband says, "Honey, you left the cap off the toothpaste again this morning." The average spouse would answer something that starts with, "Well, *you* ..." (didn't take the trash out, left your shoes in the hall again, aren't so neat all the time, either, you know, and so on.) This is a defensive approach that says, "If you're going to make me wrong, I'll find a way to make you wrong, too!" Where does this get anyone? How does this solidify the marriage, solve the spouse's issue with the toothpaste, or provide growth in the relationship?

Remember the perceptive words of Gladys Moore:

"Making the other guy wrong does not make you right."

Listen to people argue. I think you'll find that "making the other guy wrong" is an extremely common, albeit ineffective, way of communicating. The "Tell me more" technique sounds like this.

"Honey, you left the cap off the toothpaste again this morning."

"Oh, sorry! Tell me more! What else have I been doing that has been bugging you lately? Because I love you, and if I can change some things in order to make your life more pleasant, I'd be glad to give it a shot."

Most people admit to being concerned that their spouses will produce a five-page scroll of things to be worked on and improved. Truly, I doubt that this would be the case, but if this is your fear, set a boundary. Say, "Tell me more! What are *a couple* more things I could work on?"

This is not an entirely altruistic approach. Secretly, you may be hoping that your spouse would be as open and responsive to your suggestions the next time. Wow! Think of it. Both people being willing to listen and grow ... this could revolutionize relationships.

This technique can be effective for teachers, too. Suppose a student says, "That last lesson was really boring, Mrs. Ogden." Answer: "Tell me more! What else is bugging you in class? Are there some other things I need to work on? This is valuable information for me, because I want you to be relaxed and happy in class."

Suppose your daughter says, "You aren't interested in my life." (Most moms would answer, "That's not true!" But my guess is that this will *not* lead to a mutual understanding of the problem.) How about answering, "Tell me more. Help me understand why you feel that way. What should I be doing differently?"

Or, a friend says, "That dress looks terrible on you." You respond, "Tell me more. Is it the color? The style? The length?"

Then, of course, you can always combine techniques. Suppose your friend answers, "It's the color. That color just makes your face look sallow." You could now use a neutral response, "Wow, that's really good to know!" (It probably *is* good information for you!) Or, if you happen to love the color, you could now say, "Oh, that's hard to hear, because I wear this color a lot."

WAYS TO MESS UP TELL ME MORE

People with whom I have spoken suggest that this may be the hardest technique to use without sounding sarcastic. I propose that the reason for this is that we are so fearful of having inadequacies that we are quick to be sarcastic and defensive. So this approach may take some practice. Remember though, your true intention will shine through. If you really are not threatened by criticism and are interested in growth and self improvement, that will be apparent in your tone of voice and general demeanor. By contrast, if you really aren't open to suggestion, it's unlikely that you will be able to deliver this response effectively. And that would be sad.

WHEN ARE THE BEST TIMES TO USE TELL ME MORE?

This skill is best saved for use in important situations and with precious people. Use "tell me more" in the same kind of circumstance as you would use "I" messages. They are best employed where the relationship and the issue involved are both valuable and ongoing. Imagine how weird it would be to say "tell me more" after someone on the freeway criticizes your driving prowess! Obviously, time is an important ingredient here, too, as you need to be willing, and have the time, to hear the other person's continuing suggestions.

ADMINISTRATOR: Fred, great to have you back at school.

FRED: Suspension isn't that fun. I thought it would be great to be home and watch TV and stuff, but my mom made me do housework. I don't like to vacuum. And I got real bored.

ADMINISTRATOR: I'm not surprised. I think school is a pretty fun place to be!

FRED: Yeah, unless kids are calling you fat and leaving you out of football games and tattling to Mrs. Valdez about stuff you didn't even do.

ADMINISTRATOR: True, that takes a lot of the fun out of school. Well, we talked last time about trying some new stuff with those kids, so are you ready to try something kind of crazy?

FRED: Guess so. What I've done so far on my own hasn't worked out so well.

ADMINISTRATOR: Do you like these guys? Do you want to be friends with them?

FRED: Well, I used to like them.

ADMINISTRATOR: So, here's an idea. It's what I call "broken record." And it would work best if you could say it to your favorite person in the group when he's alone.

FRED: Okay.

ADMINISTRATOR: Let's say that he calls you fat. You say back, "That may be, but I'd like to be your friend."

FRED: But I'm not fat!

ADMINISTRATOR: I know ... but you can just ignore that and act like you're such a healthy person you don't need to worry about being fat. Then add the part about wanting to be his friend. See, it's really hard for someone to say something mean when you have just been honest and kind to him.

FRED: What if he says, "But I don't want to be your friend!"

ADMINISTRATOR: That's the beauty of "broken record." You just repeat, a little softer each time, "That may be, but I'd like to be your friend."

FRED: You think this will work?

ADMINISTRATOR: I'm pretty sure it will, as long as you stay calm and keep your voice real soft and keep repeating that you'd like to be his friend. It may take a little while for it to sink in, but the great thing is that you will have responded in a strong and brave way, without "getting into it" with him.

FRED: What if it doesn't work?

ADMINISTRATOR: Well, then there are two possibilities. Either he's not a nice enough kid to make a very good friend, or we can try something else.

FRED: What else can we try?

ADMINISTRATOR: Well, you could say, "Tell me more! What else is bugging you about me?"

FRED: What if he says a whole bunch of stuff?

ADMINISTRATOR: Good question. I used to worry about this when I would say that to my wife. She told me that I left the cap off the toothpaste and I said, "Tell me more, honey. What else have I been doing that is bothering you?" She came up with a big long list! So now I say, "Tell me more, Honey. Give me a couple of other things I could work on."

FRED: I'm not sure I want to hear a lot of things that he doesn't like about me.

ADMINISTRATOR: I know what you mean. But it's so healthy to admit that you might have weaknesses and that you're willing to work on them, that the other guy probably won't stay after you.

FRED: Hmmm ... I think I'll try "broken record."

ADMINISTRATOR: Sure. Good luck. I'm pretty sure that if you do it like we talked about it will work for you. But if you need some more ideas, or if at any time you think any one of those kids might get violent, come back and see me right away!

FRED: Okay, thanks.

Other Effective Responses

Other techniques that are difficult to categorize or name can be useful in responding to putdowns or avoiding power struggles. It can also be appropriate to combine a couple of techniques that have been described previously.

All of these techniques are effective because they show maturity, vulnerability, honesty, compassion, or some other indescribable wonderful trait that will cause the critical person to flee. The implied message in these is that the harasser really does care about people. It's pretty hard for people to admit that they willingly want to hurt someone or be unkind. Eventually, after hearing this powerful implied message, he will realize that cheap shots make him feel too guilty, so they just don't work with you!

SOME EXAMPLES:
- Jim Fay teaches this one: "Were you trying to hurt me? Well, you succeeded!" (Why does this work? Remember, the other guy's goal isn't really to hurt you. It's to meet his own needs.)
- "Oh, that didn't feel kind. Were you trying to be unkind?"
- "I was wondering, are you saying that because I have been unkind at some time to you?"
- "You're telling me a lot about yourself right now ..."
- "Nice try!"
- "Wow, that felt like a putdown. Is that what you intended?"
- "Am I overly sensitive, or was that meant to hurt me?"

A great one to use with students or children: "What's going on in your life right now that would cause you to say something like that?" (Implied message: something must be terribly wrong to cause you to be mean to someone else.)

I used this one once with a boy in class who was openly critical about another group of students. I pulled him out in the hall and asked what was going on in his life that would cause him to say what he said. He answered the ubiquitous, "I don't know!" So I tossed him some "either-or" questions. "Are you having trouble at home? With friends? In school? Or is something else going on?"

He quickly answered, "It's school. In fact, it's this class. I hate French!"

"Oh, are you afraid you won't do well?"

"Yes, I always struggle in French and get really low grades!"

"Oh, well, I can help you with that. If you'll just let me know when things are getting tough and you don't understand, I'll be happy to help. But the putdowns in class aren't okay. I just knew that there must have been something weird going on with you to cause you to say something like that." (The powerful implied message here is that something must be terribly amiss to cause you to be cruel to others.)

"Okay, thanks!"

I was surprised how quickly he admitted that it was his fear of failure that actually was the problem.

Try a multiple-choice question: "Did you intend to hurt me, or did that just come out wrong, or is something going on with you today ... or ...?

This is a Jim Fay technique that helps a person find an answer for a difficult question. If you just ask, "Why did you do that?" The person is likely to answer, "I don't know." Giving them a choice directs the conversation much more effectively. If the putdown was unintentional, this also gives the person an "out."

There are probably thousands of other ways to respond to taunting and harassment. A fear-free mind has the ability to find them!

In this book, you've read about many effective strategies for handling putdowns and criticism ...

... BUT WHAT HAPPENS WHEN YOU FORGET ALL THE STRATEGIES AND "MESS UP?"

I'm certain that all of us have had times when we have had the best of intentions but have not handled a situation well. This often seems to occur with people with whom we have a history of negative interactions, sometimes even a lifetime pattern. We get angry, defensive, or try to prove the other guy wrong. I find that this happens to me when the other person has really hit a nerve or when I have a strong emotional attachment to an issue or a situation. It also occurs when I'm blindsided, when I'm tired, stressed, or in a bad mood. *Often it's when the other guy is right and what he is saying is true,* and I'm just not ready to deal with my inadequacies, a new opinion, or the reality he's offering. What happens when you mess up *and you know better?*

I had this experience not long ago. I shared with a friend how I had snapped at someone, had become very argumentative and downright nasty! My friend reminded me that I had lectured to thousands of people about how *not* to respond like this. She mentioned, too, that I was writing a book on the subject. I knew this. She made great points. So I asked myself, "What is a good way to handle my guilt and the mess that I've made?" Here are some of my conclusions, in case you ever find yourself in a similar situation:

1. The best place to begin is to forgive yourself. You're doing the best you can. We're all human beings and are sure to make mistakes.

2. Then, without punishing and castigating yourself, vow to do better next time. It's a given that life will offer you another opportunity for practice, often with the same difficult person.

3. If possible and appropriate, apologize to your victim for your bad behavior. (That's a great idea. It takes a very healthy person to apologize.)

4. Develop a plan, or prepare an effective, non-defensive response to be used in case there is a similar situation in the future.

5. Then, spend a little time pondering why you were so sensitive in this scenario. Why was it that when your button was pushed you allowed it to ring your bell? The answer could reveal a great deal about the areas in which you still respond with fear. Release your fear of being inadequate or rejected, and hope for another opportunity where you can choose a better reaction.

There are two ways to approach change. Some people can *think themselves into a different way of acting.* In other words, they release all their fear and refuse to think in a defensive, angry or threatened way in the future. That way, the appropriate responses come automatically.

However, human attitudes and behaviors do not normally change all at one time. So, many people prefer to *act themselves into a different way of thinking.* When faced with a challenging situation, they choose a healthy and kind way of reacting, thus increasing their good feelings about themselves. As they continue to change each response, eventually their way of viewing life will inevitably change, also.

I believe that this will be the most viable approach for most people. We don't need to worry about transforming our total reality all at one time. When Mother Teresa was asked how she actually intended to stamp out poverty and illness in India, she responded:

"We change the world one, by one, by one ..."

We just need to concentrate on our next response.
We can change our lives one response at a time.

DAVID: Mom, I blew it today. Someone called me a "Chink," and I really got into it with him. I did all the things you have been teaching me not to. It just really hit me wrong when he said it, and I did exactly what he hoped. I got mad, retaliated, defended myself, swore, and I would have probably hit him if a teacher hadn't come up.

PARENT: Son, we've all done that many times in life! Give yourself a break. Just decide to do better next time. Remember, life is a process. It's all about making choices and learning from them.

DAVID: Yeah, I just feel really bad because I made such a fool of myself and did just what he wanted me to do.

PARENT: I have to admit that I've done that many times, too! You know, I was reading something in *Parade Magazine* today that really struck a note with me. Would you like to hear it?

DAVID: Sure.

PARENT: There was a story about a Chinese-American boy like you who was walking home from school. A car full of kids yelled "Damn Jew!" at him as they passed. At first, the boy was really angry and irritated, until it dawned on him what they had actually said. He realized that it wasn't a personal insult because he wasn't Jewish. He figured that they had just seen his dark hair and had made an assumption. Once he realized that it wasn't truly directed at him, he concluded that the kids just wanted to be hurtful, and that the racism he experienced *wasn't personal.* It wasn't even directed at him! He discovered that the message was really about the racists and their issues. The kid in the story really got some peace of mind when he realized this.

DAVID: That's pretty helpful. I forget to look at it that way sometimes. So what should I have answered when he called me a "Chink?"

PARENT: Well, you could use just about any of the techniques we've talked about ... or you could try, "Were you trying to hurt me? Well, you succeeded!"

DAVID: And that works because he wasn't really trying to hurt me?

PARENT: Exactly. He was just trying to gain some power or impress his friends, or vent some frustration from his day, or stir something up. You know, racial harassment is a great way to get a huge issue going on in a school. It's usually an effective way for a kid who feels powerless to generate some muscle.

DAVID: Uh huh.

PARENT: Or you could say, "Nice try." Or, "You're telling me a lot about yourself right now ..." Or, "I was wondering, are you saying that because I have been unkind to you at some time?"

DAVID: Lots of things to pick from.

PARENT: Yep, the key is to remember that even though it's a racial slur and very inappropriate, the same rules we've been talking about still apply. It's about the other guy and his issues, *not you!*

DAVID: I get it. I think the reason I responded so poorly today was because I'd had a tough day at school. I just wasn't in the mood.

PARENT: It's good that you've thought about that. It should make it easier for you next time to keep your cool.

DAVID: Thanks, Mom.

PARENT: Any time.

APPROACHING CHANGE

I've presented the concepts contained in this book to literally thousands of people—students of all ages, teachers, counselors, administrators, parents and professionals in other fields. Those who use them will almost always be greeted with success. They will feel proud of themselves for thinking before they react, and even prouder for being in control of themselves and their responses. It feels good, too, to refrain from anger. And of course, there is tremendous benefit in not allowing our feelings to be hurt at the whim of bullies.

But often I hear people say, "I can't remember to do the things you suggest" or "It sounds great on paper, but it's so hard to apply when the problem is occurring." I've heard middle school students say, "It's hard to do! I remember later what I should have thought about the situation and what I should have said."

Unfortunately, the model presented in America is often not one of controlling our minds, applying compassion, and personal responsibility. Tune in to our television sitcoms, soap operas, talk or reality shows. Listen to parents harshly scolding their children in the supermarket. Check out how people handle a rude driver during rush hour. It becomes obvious that the common reaction to difficult people and situations is retaliation, sarcasm, anger, and even violence.

Because humans learn primarily through imitation or modeling the behavior they see around them, it's not hard to understand why some children have adopted the nasty behaviors listed above. Any kindergarten teacher can tell you that some five year olds are already swearing and being critical and mean to other children. They are just imitating the adult models they have seen. By middle school, for many, it has become habit.

Isn't it interesting that our first response to challenging situations is normally unkind rather than loving? I've heard frustrated cab drivers in Mexico say to the person who cut them off in traffic, "Friend, why did you do that?" I have noticed, however, that in America, "friend" is not usually the noun we use to begin that sentence.

The issue, therefore, becomes how to make a permanent and positive change in our behavior. How do we break habits? How do we reject negative models and behave in more compassionate ways? We need to move from automatic, negative, or angry responses to more thoughtful and loving ways of handling situations.

Consider that when learning a new skill, we begin as unconsciously unskilled. We don't know the skill, but that's no problem, because we don't even know it exists. The next step is that we are introduced to the skill. We become consciously unskilled. We now know about the skill, but we don't know how to do it. It may be very hard to do at first. With desire and practice, we become consciously skilled. We can apply the new information, but it takes effort and thought. It may even feel awkward or uncomfortable. Sometimes, as addressed in the last chapter, we forget. We revert to our unskilled behavior. We need to go back to the drawing board, renewing our dedication to mastering the skill. The practice must continue.

With repetition (sometimes we need a great deal of it), we eventually become unconsciously skilled. That means that the new behavior will become our automatic response, which will happen with very little effort.

This is the same pattern that occurs when we learn a sport.

1. Unconsciously Unskilled
We've never heard of tennis. Mom enrolls us in a lesson.

2. Consciously Unskilled

Whew! We learn that there is a whole world of tennis stuff out there, and we don't know how to do any of it. We start with a forehand. How is the racket held? What happens with the feet? What is this thing about follow-through? Will we ever learn how to do this?

3. Consciously Skilled

We practice. We begin to learn how to hit a forehand. It takes concentration and effort. We hit hundreds of forehands. Maybe more! We hit many balls into the net. We practice more. (Imagine how many drills professional tennis players use in attempting to perfect this stroke!)

4. Unconsciously Skilled

Eventually, without even thinking about it, we effortlessly hit a great forehand.

It's interesting that with sports, dance, art, playing the piano, or other skills, we readily accept that a great deal of practice will be necessary in becoming adept at the skill. Oddly, with personal skills, many people feel that they should be able to learn them instantaneously. Not so! Like any other skill, great ability comes from desire and practice. Skill is usually a result of repetition and effort.

So it is with learning to use our minds well. I believe that the first step is to realize that an individual does indeed possess the power to use his mind as he intends to.

Let's try an experiment. Picture in your mind a yellow giraffe with black spots. Now switch your visual to a purple cow. Can you do it? Can you visualize both animals? Then you are the one operating your mind. You are telling it what to think!

It's no different in learning how to think and respond to putdowns or criticism. The process is the same as the one you used to visualize the giraffe and the cow. We can choose how we are going to think. We can break the habit of retaliating or feeling hurt. We can choose to feel sad for the person who is being mean. We can then use any of the skills or statements presented in this book to respond in a way which does not fan the fires of discord and anger.

The most positive benefit might be that we learn that we have a choice in how we use our minds. We can choose how we think about people and situations. It is a discipline that can be developed and improved with practice until it becomes easy and automatic. Imagine how skillful children could become at using their minds in a positive way if we begin teaching them at a young age the potential they have, while encouraging them to use and develop their ability. What an incredible power to harness!

STAYING ON TRACK

Now that we know a more positive way to think and react, how do we stick to it? How do we internalize it?

In the last chapter, we discussed what to do when we respond inappropriately. As with any behavior change, it is easy to relapse into old patterns of thinking and behaving. But how do we raise the odds of that not happening? How do we help our children stay on track?

The following are a few suggestions for how to help kids develop an entirely new set of behaviors, and how to help them respond effectively every time. These ideas can help them become "unconsciously skilled."

1. Model how to respond and react to bullies and critics

Talk out loud about how you handle the difficult situations and people you encounter. You might say, "I'm going to choose to not worry about the nasty comment said to me today. Instead, I'm going to remember that the person who said it was probably having a tough day. Something bad must have been going on with her. How sad! I did tell her that her comment hurt my feelings, and I feel good about that. I didn't get angry or say something mean back to her. I'm proud of myself!"

2. Use quotes

They can be of tremendous help as they summarize complicated ideas in succinct ways. There are so many opportunities to connect quotes to real life situations. Challenge yourself to find times during the day when these quotes apply to what you're experiencing, and then share these discoveries with your child. Next, you might invite your child to play the same game, asking him to apply these quotes to situations in *his* life. Here are two that I think are very powerful and appropriate for this purpose:

> *"Hurt people hurt people."*
> *"When I am angry at myself, I criticize others."*
> *Ed Howe*

Don't forget some of the quotes previously mentioned in this book, for example:

> *"No one can make you feel inferior without your permission."* *Eleanor Roosevelt*

> *"When someone pushes your button, don't let it ring your bell."*

> *"Never act as small as the other guy feels."* *Jim Fay*

You might like to review the other quotes in the book, then pick out the ones that resonate with you and your child. Put them in places that jog your thinking. How about putting a sticky note on the refrigerator, on the mirror, on top of the computer, where your child does his homework, or slipped into his lunchbox?

As these sayings become familiar to your child, use the first part only, making a game of it. The goal is to incorporate these ideas into the child's repertoire until the concepts become a part of who he is.

Say, "Hurt people ..." "Never act as small ..." and let your child finish the quote for himself.

3. Initiate some key words.

Work together with your child to select some words which "kick in" the new thought processes and information. These key words are designed as a shortcut to switch the thinking from the old pattern to the new concept.

For example, to remind your child that he has the power to adjust his thinking and choose his thoughts, you might simply use the word "giraffe." (Remember when we visualized a giraffe, then changed to a purple cow?) Or, to remind your child that he can out-crazy the crazies, say, "Banana!"

4. Teach your child to use one technique at a time.

Repeat this phrase often, "I'm sorry you feel that way!" Quiz him. "What do you say when someone says something nasty to you? That's right, "I'm sorry you feel that way."

5. Invite your child to teach a friend what he has learned.

Research tells us that one of the most effective ways to internalize information is to teach others. This is another technique that can help this information stick permanently in your child's mind.

Conclusion

There are profound benefits to be gained by using the information presented in this book. Shifting perspectives and changing to more loving responses have the potential of radically improving relationships. First we can improve the quality of our own lives and the lives of others, and eventually we can decrease violence in the world, thereby increasing world peace! We can change how we interpret the cruel and thoughtless actions of others. We can change how we think about those actions, and we can change how we choose to respond. Although it takes some practice, it is not a complicated process.

Dr. Wayne Dyer affirms that change is possible by offering this thought from *Staying on the Path:*

"You don't have to continue to behave the way you have behaved, just because you always have."

It is self-transformational to learn how to think and respond kindly and effectively to nasty people, derogatory comments, and potentially volatile situations. It preserves and increases our belief in ourselves. When we make the switch to believing that we don't have to please everyone, and that it is okay to have weaknesses and make mistakes, a whole new world opens for us. It is a world in which we can forgive ourselves, take risks and grow. In this world we can treat others with kindness and compassion. It feels good to be loving. And the more we believe in and value ourselves, the kinder we are toward others. It becomes a loving, *non-vicious cycle.*

Don't forget Lincoln's words:

"When I do good, I feel good. I do bad, I feel bad."

In addition, we will develop a peace of mind that can come from understanding and translating the actions of others, feeling sadness or compassion for their situation, and releasing our own fear of being inadequate or rejected. This peace of mind is a magnificent gift to give to ourselves! Compassion is a marvelous gift to give others.

The more loving we are toward others, the better they feel about themselves. Positive interactions and friendships help us define ourselves as valuable and lovable human beings. In the book, *The Art of Happiness,* the Dalai Lama is quoted as saying:

> **"If you approach others with the thought of compassion, that will automatically reduce fear and allow an openness with other people. It creates a positive, friendly atmosphere."**

The Dalai Lama also asserts:

> **"Since at the beginning and end of our lives we are completely dependent on the kindness of others, how can it be that in the middle we would neglect kindness toward others?"**

In addition, if we are dedicated to increasing the love and decreasing the violence in our society, we must *model* for others that it is possible to respond to critical, antagonistic behavior with integrity, wisdom and compassion. Albert Schweitzer stated:

"Example is not the main thing in influencing others; it is the only thing."

It is no wonder that our society is so vengeful and aggressive. One has only to look at the model presented in movies and on TV. The winner usually overpowers his guy with brute force. Retaliation is the norm. Violence appeals at the box office and nastiness among main characters is common. Look at the popularity of Jerry Springer and similar shows! I believe that we must begin to combat this example by modeling a much more loving and healthy way of behaving. It may seem to be an overwhelming task. However, it's not beneficial to believe that it is formidable. Many great philanthropists have proven that great change is indeed possible.

When we learn to respond appropriately and with kindness to ourselves and others in these types of situations, we assist ourselves and others in transforming our world to a more loving and peaceful one. Shakti Gawain states:

"The most powerful thing you can do to change the world is to change your own beliefs about the nature of life, people, reality, to something more positive ... and begin to act accordingly."

Gandhi adds:

"You must be the change you wish to see in the world."

Deepak Chopra sums it up beautifully:

"When you transform yourself, the world you live in will also be transformed."

The possible end result could be world peace! I am a little given to exaggeration, and it's possible that world peace could be a little more complex, but surely it begins here.

Deepak Chopra also inspires with this thought:

"Together we can dream a new world into reality."

Wayne Dyer, in the book, *Staying on the Path*, adds:

If others hurt you, let the injury go;
If you let it go, you will find serenity.

Good luck. Try it! Take a risk! Change your perspective!

Get out there and get put down ... then use one of these responses and ways of thinking, and watch for the magical results!

Go for it! Life's pretty fun, no?

"Take yourself to the edge of what you know, and throw yourself off!" Release your fear! Use some new skills!

And next time you find yourself in a tough situation or with a difficult person, choose to use your mind in a loving and powerful way, reflect on the information in this book and say to yourself,

"Words will NEVER hurt me!"

SUGGESTED READING AND RECOMMENDED RESOURCES

Chopra, Deepak, M.D. *Unconditional Life*. New York, New York: Bantam Books: 1991.

Dyer, Wayne. *Staying on the Path*. Carson, California: Hay House, Inc., 1995.

Dyer, Wayne. *Real Magic*. New York, New York: Harper Paperbacks, 1992.

Dyer, Wayne. *Pulling Your Own Strings*. New York, New York: Harper Books, 1978.

Dyer, Wayne. *You'll See it When you Believe It*. New York, New York: Avon Books, 1990.

Dyer, Wayne. *Your Erroneous Zones*. New York, New York: Harper Perennial, 1991.

Fay, Jim & Funk, David. *Teaching With Love and Logic*. Golden, Colorado: The Love and Logic Press, Inc., 1995.

Gawain, Shakti. *Living in the Light*. San Rafael, California: Whatever Publishing, Inc., 1986.

Gawain, Shakti. *The Path of Transformation*. Mill Valley, California: Nataraj Publishing, 1993.

Gawain, Shakti. *Creating True Prosperity*. Novato, California: New World Library, 1997.

Gordon, Thomas E. *Parent Effectiveness Training*. New York, New York: Crown Publishing Group, 2000.

Gordon, Thomas E. *Teacher Effectiveness Training*. New York, New York: David McKay, 1974.

His Holiness the Dalai Lama and Cutler, Howard C. M.D. *The Art of Happiness*. New York, New York: Riverhead Books, 1998.

His Holiness the Dalai Lama. *Ethics for the New Millennium*. New York, New York: Riverhead Books, 1999.

REFERENCES

Bushman, B. J., Baumeister, R. F., Phillips, C. M. (in press). "Do people aggress to improve their Mood? Catharsis beliefs, affect regulation opportunity, and aggressive responding." *Journal of Personality and Social Psychology*, March 1999.

Goode, Erica. "Letting Out Aggression Is Called Bad Advice." *The New York Times Science Tuesday*, March 1999.

Gross, Amy. "A Perscription for Happiness"—An interview with Sharon Salzberg. *American Health Magazine*, April 1998, p. 32.

Keelan, James. *B. S.* and Live Longer (*Beat Stress)*. Arvada, Colorado: 1978.

Klein, Edward. "Jackie Triumphant", (adapted from the book, *Just Jackie: Her Private Years*). *People Magazine.* October 1998, p.135.

Minton, Lynn. "A Racial Slur Opened My Eyes." *Parade Magazine.* July 16, 2000, p. 15.

Tavris, Carol. *Anger: The Misunderstood Emotion.* Old Tappan, New Jersey: Simon & Schuster Trade, 1989.